LIZ MOHN

Love Opens Hearts

Liz Mohn

Love Opens
Hearts

Recorded by
Madlen Hildebrecht

Translated from the German by
Helga Schier

Love Opens Hearts

Translation copyright © 2001 by Helga Schier

All rights reserved under International and Pan-American Copyright Conventions.
Published in the United States by Random House, Inc., New York, and simultaneously
in Canada by Random House of Canada Limited, Toronto. Originally published in
German as *Liebe öffnet Herzen* by C. Bertelsmann in 2001. Copyright © 2001
by C. Bertelsmann.

Library of Congress Cataloging-in-Publication data
Mohn, Liz.
[Liebe öffnet Herzen. English]
Love opens hearts / Liz Mohn ; recorded by Madlen Hildebrecht ;
translated from the German by Helga Schier.
p. cm.
ISBN 0-375-42572-1
1. Mohn, Liz. 2. Germany—Biography. 3. Bertelsmann Stiftung (Gütersloh,
Germany) 4. Women philanthropists—Germany—Biography. 5. Human
services—Germany. 6. Charities—Germany. 7. Verlagsgruppe Bertelsmann.
I. Hildebrecht, Madlen. II. Title.
AS911.A4 B47613 2001
305.4'092—dc21
[B]   2001048463

www.randomhouse.com

Typeset and printed in the United States of America

10   9   8   7   6   5   4   3   2

First American Edition

Dedicated to my husband Reinhard—
my best teacher,
the single most important influence on my life and
    my thinking,
my partner in life—
to you, a token of thanks.

Table of Contents

1. Beginnings—Roots

The limousine hums along the country road. From the back of the car, I watch the lush green of the trees fly by. It is one of those spring days that make your heart leap—bright sunshine, deep blue skies, fields full of buttercups and rapeseed as yellow as egg yolk. Lost in thought, I watch the beauty of nature unfold. I'm on my way to a self-help group of the German Stroke Foundation. This area is so familiar to me. Far below lies the bed of the river Ems, a river that has been close to me since I was a small child. One place is particularly dear to me, a place where willows hang deep into the water.

"Please be so kind as to stop for a moment." My driver, Thomas Barnhöfer, nods in recognition—he knows how important this place is to me. We've stopped here many times before.

I go down to the river bank and watch my reflection in the water. Memories of long-passed days appear before my eyes. I see a little blond girl running, grabbing hold of a willow branch, and swinging over to the other side of the river bank. What great fun! Again and again she swings back and forth. Sometimes, with luck, she makes it safely to the other side. Sometimes she doesn't. When she falls into the water, she just spits it out, shakes herself off, and starts all over again.

I am that little girl. I couldn't swim then. This is how I learned—I taught myself. I was four years old at the time. Later my mother told me that this was when she caught the first glimpse of my strength and my courage.

This place is part of my roots. Every so often I need these memories. They give me renewed strength for my work. It's been a long journey from that stubborn little girl to the woman I am today. I return to my car in a reflective mood. The members of the self-help group are waiting for me.

"Are you okay, Mrs. Mohn?" Thomas Barnhöfer asks while opening the door for me. I just nod. He's been my driver for many years, and we know each other well. We don't need many words to communicate. While we continue our drive, I reminisce over the lost world of my childhood.

I was born during a time when death and destruction reigned supreme. On the battlefields of Europe the lives of millions were coming to a close—and yet my life had just begun. We are all part of the eternal circle of life and death. As a child of war, my chances for a happy and successful life were slim—just like those of all the other newborns at the time. All that mattered was survival. The women who gave birth in those days, who protected their children and kept them safe, who sacrificed themselves to raise them, are still heroes to me. My mother would later tell me that I was born during an air raid, on the eve of the war with Russia. Germany lay under a spell of fear. That fear consumed my mother when I was born: fear for her own life, fear for the life of her child. Worry about an uncertain future. It was as if this fear had been passed on to me. Later I heard and read a lot about how children sense a mother's emotions, moods and fears in the womb. This is what must have happened to us, because I was a fearful baby. I constantly cried at night, plagued by nightmares. Every night my mother had to pick me up and comfort me. Perhaps this is why the two of us have always had an especially strong bond.

Like many children of my generation, I have nothing but scattered memories of the war. Yet to this day I can taste the fear that came with it. We lived through many air raids in Wiedenbrück. The actual targets of the bomber planes, Bielefeld and the Ruhr area, were nearby. Bombs would fall as close as the outskirts of our town. At night we children were often torn from our beds to run to the safety of the bunker. I'll never forget how afraid I was, running along the street, clinging to my mother's hand, accompanied only by the screams of air-raid sirens. I'll never forget the stuffy smell of the narrow basement full of frightened men, women, and children, huddling close to each other in the dim light, breathing in the stale air.

One morning when we returned home from the bunker, my bed was full of frost. Everything was frozen. Icy flowers spread themselves over our windows, proof that we didn't have any heat in our house. To make sure we wouldn't be cold, my mother heated up bricks in the oven and put them in our beds. It was so cozy. This feeling is with me to this day.

When I think about my childhood and my youth, I remember love and care. But the world around us was in ruins. Hunger, misery, and need were everywhere. Yet as a child, I was mercifully unaware of the implications of what was happening around us. We lived simply, but we were a family full of trust and a sense of safety. This feeling is still with me. This tells me that, for children, true happiness doesn't come from beautiful clothes, expensive toys, or travels to faraway lands. True happiness for children is being loved and feeling secure. We were loved at home, a lot, and we were safe. My mother made sure of that.

I know that material things cannot provide any meaning to life. A car, a beautiful house, or professional success cannot replace a gentle hug. Love, tenderness, and trust cannot be found in material goods or expensive gifts. Love, tenderness, and trust can only be found in the comfortable and comforting embraces of people dear to you.

Our mother took care of us night and day. She rented a small garden to grow vegetables and potatoes so that we'd have enough to eat. I still remember the sour taste of her bread soup, served for lunch so many times. Bread soup was one of the major food sources in the years immediately following the war. Like many other children at the time, after a while I wanted neither to smell nor eat this soup. But hunger got the better of me, and I choked it down anyway. Hunger wasn't as much of a problem in the country as it was in the cities. In our small town people shared everything. If someone in the neighborhood slaughtered a pig, everybody could partake. As children we would often go with our mother to collect beechnuts to press oil, or go to the woods to collect firewood. In the morning we would have to pluck bugs from the potatoes in the garden. I remember all too well how disgusted I was when they started crawling up my arms.

Children of my generation didn't know boredom or weariness. All families had to struggle simply to survive and to make ends meet. No one, not even children, was spared from this struggle.

My Mother

My mother was one of nine children. She was a skilled hat maker. My father's background was that of a farmer, and later he trained to become a craftsman. He had to overcome great misfortune. He was hit by lightning, and he had to be hospitalized for two weeks before finally regaining consciousness. But he was never again fit for work, which is why he was never drafted. This was very hard on him, because I think he believed it was dishonorable. This kind of thinking was typical for the times. He was only 60 years old when he passed away.

All five of us children related to my mother more than anyone else. She assumed all the family's responsibilities. Today you would say that she was a strong woman who made all her decisions on her own. At the time this seemed quite natural. Today a woman like my mother would be seen as a woman with a strong personality. But in those days women played the hand they were dealt without any discussion. This doesn't mean, of course, that these women didn't feel the emotional and physical strain all the same.

My mother was always there for us. She cooked. She did laundry. She made our clothes. Naturally we noticed that it wasn't easy on her, even though we were only children. It was obvious that she had to think twice about every penny she spent. And her worries about our future didn't go unnoticed either. Even as a very small child I could sense when something was bothering her. I would take her hand and caress it. I wanted to comfort her as best I could. I loved her very much.

She was, all in all, a cheerful person, despite the hard times she had. She was a slender woman with black hair and blue eyes that looked upon the world with a lively curiosity. Her motto was: Don't let things get you down. My mother always tried to think positively. She always had a song on her lips. Her many friends and acquaintances would often stop by, so our house was always full of visitors. She never had a mean word for anyone. Instead, she had a big heart, with room for all. She tried to help whomever she could, whenever she could.

In the years immediately after the war many people had nothing to eat, so they turned to panhandling. My mother would always find something to give when someone came knocking at our door—a piece of bread, a few vegetables, a bowl of soup. Children from the Ruhr area would spend their summers with us, and she would feed them while nourishing them with more than just food. I don't know how she did it, but she made so many things possible for us. We had bicycles and roller skates and ice skates. We loved to play on the banks of the river Ems. In the summer months we'd bathe in the river, and in the winter months we'd skate on its frozen surface. When we came home, chilled as icicles, she would greet us with doughnuts from the oven. Things were always so cozy when she was around, and yet I only could fully appreciate what she did for us once I had children of my own. The world she created was safe; full of tenderness, love, and care.

In those days she drew much of her strength from God; in her old age, however, religion didn't mean that much to her any more.

My mother loved people. I learned this from her. She shaped me in so many ways, more than I was ready to admit when I was younger. Only later, as an adult mother of three children and a professional woman with people depending on me, was I finally able to see and acknowledge her influence.

My optimism and positive outlook on life are most likely hers as well. She was an adventurous woman even into old age. When she was 88 years old, she came to visit us in our house on Mallorca. She loved the view from our terrace, but after a while she remarked, "Just sitting here and watching the ocean is rather boring." She wanted to do something, to go to town, to be among people.

My mother lived to be 94 years old. When she died, rather than being grief-stricken, I was grateful instead for what she had given me. I had said my farewell to her earlier, during her long years of illness. Being able to say good-bye made the pain easier for me to bear. I hope that, when the time comes, my children will have enough time to say good-bye to me. I had my mother's coffin covered with red and white orchids. They were her favorite flowers.

A Brave Little Girl

We were five children altogether, and I was the fourth. I was closest to my sister Hannelore, who was three years older, and to my brother Heinz, who was five years older, because our ages were compatible. But my other sister was five years younger than me. I wasn't thrilled when she was born; I was jealous, because I was afraid that I'd have to share my mother's love.

Looking back upon the child I once was, I see a little girl with blond ponytails, who was so slender and delicate that her mother always seemed to worry. She wanted me to eat more than my brothers and sisters, and I asked for and needed more of my mother's help and attention. I was a needy and timid child—quite different from my siblings. I think that's why my mother and I had a special bond. My mother knew all my fears. Fear of going down into a dark basement. Fear of new situations. Fear of challenges. I needed a lot of encouragement.

On the other hand, if I set my mind to do something, nothing could stop me. In such moments I would find a willpower in me

I had never even imagined. It gave me courage to go beyond my fears and to embark on new adventures. Bertholt Brecht once said that courage is part and parcel of talent. I think this fits my development to a tee.

In first grade I was the only one who dared to jump off the high dive. After all my training in the river Ems, I had become quite an accomplished swimmer. My teacher encouraged me to take the plunge. He simply said, "Why don't you try it? You can do it!" I sensed that he believed in me. I remember every single thing that went through my mind while climbing the ladder fifteen feet up to the springboard. I climbed higher and higher, as if going straight to heaven. My heart was pounding. My knees were shaking. When I finally arrived up on top and saw my schoolmates and my teacher down below, looking up expectantly, there was no turning back. I jumped. Afterwards I felt very proud of myself.

There were several other moments like that in my life. Whenever I sensed that someone believed in me, I was able to overcome my fears. Throughout my life I have been blessed with people who would encourage me to go forward and take the next step. Today, in my work, I always try to encourage my coworkers, drawing on the lessons of my own early experiences. And eventually, by the way, I even did a somersault from that high dive!

I continued to love the water, and I became a swimmer with great stamina. These days, it isn't all that difficult for me to swim comfortably in the Mediterranean, while talking, for up to an hour. Our company's managers, on the other hand, on visits to our vacation home on Mallorca, may have to catch their breath every once in a while just trying to keep up with me!

As a child I lived in my own world. I was friendly, but somewhat dreamy once in a while. At night I could often be found sitting on the windowsill in the kitchen, singing songs. I would sneak out of bed and go for a walk at five in the morning; I loved walking in the meadows when the grass was wet with dew. I would run along the Ems until I reached the nearby forest, where I would listen to the birds singing their early morning song to the accompaniment of trees rustling in the wind. It was like a dream . . . my own little adventure.

I've always felt an intuitive connection with nature. I still feel this closeness today. When I feel lonely, when I'm not sure what to do next, when I'm under a lot of stress, that's when I seek out nature. I go for long walks in the meadows, the woods, or the mountains. I usually walk at a rather brisk pace, breathing deeply, filled with joy in the vastness of the Münster valley that stretches all the way to the horizon. It usually doesn't take long to feel calm and serene again.

It's on these walks that I can collect my thoughts and separate what's important from what's not. We humans are only small cogs in the larger machine. I can see that when I look at an ancient oak tree, wondering about the stories such a tree could tell. Some people travel to India in search of serenity to center themselves. Others go to a cloister to meditate. I find that center in nature. There, the wind that caresses my face has been blowing for two thousand years, when the Romans were fighting the Cherusci in the nearby Teutoburg Forest.

It's at these times that the fragility of human existence becomes crystal clear to me, and I can stop taking myself so seriously. Happiness begins in your head. So I decided not to let external circumstances influence my inner life. I am very glad that I never lost sight of the smaller things in life. I'm still able to enjoy a beautiful flower, a sunset over the ocean, the view of majestic mountain ranges, someone's smile, and the comfort of a conversation with a good, trusted friend.

Decisive Years:
School and Scouts[1]

My first day of school was difficult. I was consumed by fear. It was the very first time that I found myself separated from my mother,

[1] The *Pfadfinder* (Pathfinders) are a German organization similar to the Boy/Girl Scouts.

and I felt vulnerable and exposed. I remember clearly how frightened I was, sitting there in the first row, looking up at the teacher, Mrs. Verhoff. Mrs. Verhoff was an older woman. It was a stroke of luck that she ended up being my teacher, because she was able to handle us first graders warmly, almost like a mother. She was the one who helped me get past my fears very quickly. The scared little girl full of trepidation grew into a self-assured little girl full of smiles who got along well with every one of her teachers, because she managed to steal their hearts.

Years later, after having lived in Gütersloh for a while, and a few years into Mrs. Verhoff's retirement, I happened to see her at a bus stop as I drove by in a car. I stopped and offered her a ride, but she didn't quite recognize me at first. Then we talked about my early school years, and I thanked her belatedly for all the helpful comfort her care and generosity had given me during that time.

I remember that I was usually the last to arrive at school, my bags always hanging open. This is because rather than doing my homework the day before, I preferred to study poetry or vocabulary at four or five in the morning before school. That was when I excelled. I found German and History interesting and fascinating. Mathematics, on the other hand, wasn't my thing. Neither were sports. I found gymnastics tedious because I wasn't strong enough. I suppose a bit of fear had something to do with it as well. It wasn't until later, under much different circumstances, that I found an appreciation for physical activities.

In the end, the conclusion I would draw from my school days is that it is not necessarily the best students who are guaranteed success. And many a beautiful girl from my school days found herself living a hard life. Beauty, knowledge, and good grades do not guarantee success in life. Other characteristics, such as a willingness to do your best, are important tools for success. Logic and rational intelligence must be paired with emotional intelligence. Stamina, discipline, energy, and diligence are vitally important as well. And a good heart and emotional health should not be forgotten either. You need the ability to approach people, inspire them, and excite them for your ideas to be successful. Now in the new millennium, as ever, self-motivation, intuition, creativity, and the ability to work as part of a team are all valuable character traits.

My effervescent temperament became apparent as I grew older, as my curiosity grew until it could no longer be curbed. Everything was interesting to me. When my mother sent me on an errand, I would find so many new and interesting things, and so many people to chat with, that I never failed to return home late.

To channel this adventurous and impulsive nature, my mother signed me up for the Pathfinders, a sort of Catholic Girl Scouts.

That was a great education for me. I learned about community life in youth hostels. To this day, my heart is still warmed by beautiful memories of campfires, trips under the starlit sky at night, singing and cooking with the caretakers of the hostels, and washing up with cold water. It was the "simple life," what travel agencies these days call "adventure tours" as a selling point. Night walks without flashlights, lit only by the moon, were especially exciting to me. And I remember our long bicycle excursions, too. I was always last to arrive at the agreed-upon destination, because I was the most delicate. Yet nobody got angry or impatient with me. On the contrary, everybody was happily considerate enough to wait for those of us who were weaker.

For me, Pathfinders was an educational program where young girls built character. We depended on one another on these trips, and everybody had to pitch in for the common good. We'd all have to help put up the tent, or light a fire with only one match, or cook, or do the dishes. Nobody was special, and nobody asked for anything out of the ordinary, because that would have thrown us off balance. This is how we learned to take responsibility for ourselves and each other, a virtue which nowadays is rarely taught or learned.

I felt safe within a group, yet I also had to learn to give up my own interests in favor of those of the group. Sometimes this meant gritting my teeth and fighting back tears. But later, when I was a little older, another girl and I led one of the girls' groups, an experience which I really enjoyed. We were supposed to be role models for the little scouts and watch out for them at the same time. After all, we were responsible for them. I still know the songs I learned in those days—I even passed them on to my own children. I had the lyrics to my favorite song ("Your Thoughts Are Free") framed for my office.

I learned something else as well. The Pathfinder motto became second nature to me: Don't let a day go by without doing a good deed. Even if all I can give is a smile, I try not to ignore other people.

When my own children were small I tried to find Girl and Boy Scout troops for them. Unfortunately, the sixties movement placed the ideals of discipline and organization, so important to the scout troops, squarely in the conservative camp. They weren't *en vogue*, and so I wasn't able to find a group for any of my children. I understand that in the last few years they have become popular again. Apparently today's parents are trying to expose their children to adventures in nature, far away from our saturated consumer mentality. Closeness to nature is an experience parents cannot teach their children in the cities.

There are thirty million Girl and Boy Scouts worldwide. I doubt that the British General Baden-Powell, who founded the movement in 1907, even dreamed of such immense success. Numerous celebrities have been members, among them almost all of the US Presidents. Some of the German members are the Governor of North-Rhine Westphalia, Wolfgang Clement, former Employment Minister Norbert Blüm, and even Thomas Gottschalk, the entertainer, as well as Christiane Herzog, the late wife of the former German President Roman Herzog.

Growing Up in a Small Town—
Tradition and Values

The history of my hometown, Wiedenbrück—a place of about eight thousand inhabitants when I was growing up—begins in the twelfth century. The outline of the medieval town still exists today. Streets with cobblestones draw a tightly knit net around the marketplace and the church square. The gabled farmers' residences prominently define the town's look. There are forty-two of them, all with carved inscriptions, built between 1500 and 1850, and all beautifully restored. Their facades, decorated with colorful ornaments carved from wood, vary in style: Renaissance, Baroque, and Classical. The huge gates of the farm manors show how important farming once was to the town's prosperity.

People knew each other in our small town. As children this gave us a sense of protection and safety. People welcomed you everywhere, and nobody was ever lost. I liked that. As children we enjoyed running through the narrow medieval streets. One of our favorite games was to try to decipher the German and Latin inscriptions on the houses. On the back of our 1619 town hall, for example, you'll find parts of the Latin inscription: ". . . war is the end. Peace is the mother of all, and the protector of things . . . not distraction, not love, not a work of religion. Peace renews everything, peace brings golden times. Peace carries with it the rules of strict simplicity." As a child it fascinated me that these were the words and thoughts of our ancestors. It gave me a sense of history, and it made me wonder what we would pass on to our children and grandchildren.

Wiedenbrück has kept its charm to this day. Our citizens are proud of their little town, and a sense of togetherness prevails. To this day I love going to our annual Christmas fair on the church square, where I have a glass of punch with old friends and chat about old times.

Wiedenbrück was a Catholic stronghold for many centuries, until a Protestant community was established there in the nineteenth century. I was raised Catholic. We went to Mass every morning at seven, before school. On Christmas we had to go even earlier, at five, and I still remember how terribly cold I was. There was no heat at home yet, and it was the same in church.

We said grace at home, but my prayer was very short: "Thank you for our supper. Amen." I never felt like saying a long prayer.

I did like our yearly Corpus Christi procession, though. I thought that was a beautiful tradition. Our entire school plucked daisies and cuckoo-flowers in the meadows, and the adults cut peonies from their gardens. We decorated all the altars along the main street. I can still smell the aroma of the freshly cut May trees "planted" along the main street that make it look like a long arbor. The girls wore white lace dresses, and we even got to wear knee-highs or socks. People everywhere came out of their houses to join the procession at the church square, where we sang "Good God, We Praise You." It was very festive, and I was always deeply touched.

Corpus Christi was a very nice tradition that gave us a sense of belonging. But there are traditions and customs other than the religious ones that I also find very important. County fairs, choral societies, and even family parties give people a sense of values, a sense of togetherness, a sense of community and comfort. I think we should cherish these traditions, rather than let them fade. They are part and parcel of our culture. Without traditions people lose their sense of history and exist in a vacuum, cut off from their roots. Those old traditions are very important to me, a small world in themselves, one that has given me a solid foundation. A sense of tradition, according to psychologists today, is important for children in order for them to develop an independent, balanced, and centered personality. And my own experience tells me that many successful managers come from a background that provided the stability of such structures.

Another important traditional structure for me was Christmastime, which is an especially fond memory for me. Christmas was a time of anticipation and joy. Often we would bake cookies with my mother, and later we would eat them in candlelight while sipping a cup of herbal tea. We would sing Christmas carols and make decorations, and then our mother would talk about the meaning of the holidays. She told us that Christmas was meant to remind us that all people deserve help, despite their errors, and that everybody would be forgiven through love.

And of course, there were presents. The one I cherished most was a handmade doll. My mother had made it from pieces of cloth. Later, of course, I was proud to finally get a "real" doll with porcelain head, complete with a cradle.

I had to earn my allowance early on. I delivered the *Dome*, a Catholic newspaper. I enjoyed this small job, and everybody knew me. People always found time for a quick chat at their door. I wasn't shy or afraid. In fact, I was open and liked to talk. I'm sure it was this sunny disposition that earned me many a tip. Thus I learned quickly that people react positively to friendliness. Early on this fixed in my mind a simple truth: You get as much as you give.

The Spirit of Adventure

As soon as I knew how to read I became a regular bookworm. I read everything I could lay my hands on: *Heidi, Treasure Island, Uncle Tom's Cabin,* and even books by Karl May, Mark Twain, and Jules Verne. I particularly enjoyed reading adventure stories. They made me so curious, these tales of far-off worlds. I wanted to know what a coconut looked like, what Brazil was like, how dangerous crocodiles really were, what the life of a missionary was like, and what American Indians were like. Secretly I promised myself that I would get to know all of this firsthand.

But first, of course, I wanted to explore Germany. My first opportunity to do so came when I went on a bike tour with my cousin. I was fourteen, very curious, and adventurous. My father had arranged for a friend of his, a truck driver, to take us as far as

Würzburg. From there we had to ride our bikes back home to Wiedenbrück. Both seasoned Pathfinders, we came prepared with tents, food, and drink.

I remember very well how my father's friend dropped us off on the side of the road. Home was to the north. But in the opposite direction was Rothenburg at the Tauber. We'd heard a lot about this romantic little town, so why not take a look before making our way back home? And then . . . off we went!

Rothenburg was nice, but there was a sign pointing to Munich. Why not continue on to Munich? Wouldn't it be nice to get to know Munich, I suggested. We were in luck. A truck driver picked us up, and then at our next stop we were at the lakes in Upper Bavaria. Then again by truck to Hamburg, and then to Helgoland on a boat called *The Colored Cow*. Our bicycles had long since turned into luggage!

This is how we toured Germany. We stopped wherever we liked, and everything was wonderful. Of course, we were cautious. We were careful to always check out the truck drivers before going with them. One of them had his children with him, so we considered him to be especially trustworthy. His children sat up front in the cab while we slept on the truck bed in back. All along our journey we sent postcards back to our parents. Obviously our route took them by surprise, but after three weeks on the road, filthy, yet exhilarated by our adventure, we finally returned home. Our parents were both glad and relieved that we had made it back safely. It was only then that we realized how much they had worried about us. We felt pretty bad about the heartache we had caused them. Overtaken by curiosity and our taste for adventure, we had thrown all caution to the wind. But that's youth . . . then, now, and forever.

This trip nourished my dream to leave the safe yet narrow world of Wiedenbrück behind. I wanted to see and experience more, and I became determined to make something of my life. Of course, I wasn't quite sure yet what I wanted to do, nor how I was going to do it. I wasn't dreaming of an exciting career. I was thinking more along the lines of a good place to work, a nice husband, and lots of children. You see, I'm an intuitive person, and my intuition has always directed me well. It isn't as if I had been consciously moving towards any specific goals, but when an opportunity presented itself, I was alert enough to recognize and grab it. That's when I was able to make quick and clear decisions. I've also always enjoyed opportunities to be with people who were different from me. I always wanted to be with people who knew something about life, people who had a different education from me, people who could teach me something.

There have been a few turning points in my life, moments of sudden clarity and realization. One of these key moments was meeting a group of students. They had a chance to do something special with their lives, something that I wanted, too. Yet I knew that you have to work for such a chance, that opportunities don't just fall into your lap, and that you have to make an effort.

I wanted that chance.

First Meeting

I'm still amazed that I actually had the courage to go to an interview at Bertelsmann. There is a story to that. My mother had set me up as an apprentice at a dentist's office. In those days, just like now, people were happy to have a place to work at all. So I started training there, even though I didn't like it. I wanted something different. A girlfriend of mine worked at Bertelsmann, and that seemed much more interesting and promising to me.

So I applied at Bertelsmann without telling my mother. The interview took place at the distribution center, and I wore my best white blouse that day. I loved white blouses. They looked so clean and fresh, and they made me feel so polished.

I walked the two and a half miles from Wiedenbrück to Rheda, where the distribution center was located. I was very nervous when I spoke with Mrs. Ehrmann, who was responsible for personnel at the time. But she had a lot of sensitivity, and I think she liked me right away. In any case, she hired me as a trainee. Her husband, by the way, was the manager of the distribution center. After the interview I could have hugged everybody. I was so proud. Somehow I could sense that life had a few surprises in store for me.

After only six weeks on the job I was invited to the yearly company party. I had to argue with my parents to be able to go at all. I wasn't allowed to go out at night, because at seventeen you weren't considered an adult yet. Children were raised differently then. But after a lot of arguing back and forth, they gave in and let me go. Of course, I was supposed to be back home by ten that night.

I remember the evening very well. I was sitting among a group of young girls, all of us trainees. I wore a white wool dress that my mother had made for me. It made me feel pretty. It was then that I first saw Reinhard Mohn, my future husband, come in with a group of people I didn't know at all. I was very curious about him, and all of us craned our necks just to catch sight of him. He stood tall. A smile played around his mouth. I found him very handsome, with a great deal of charisma.

I was completely taken by surprise when he asked me, of all people, to dance with him. It was a waltz. I don't remember what we talked about . . . probably nothing but small talk. But I do remember that I was very surprised at how charming and open he seemed to be. At one point, when playing musical chairs, it came down to just the two of us in the end, fighting for the last chair. He won.

We got along very well, and we stayed at the party until very late. He didn't take me home until five in the morning! I remember the police following us, because he was speeding. My mother was waiting up for me. Of course, she hadn't slept all night because I hadn't been home by ten as promised. To this day I feel bad that I worried her so, but I was young, open to anything new. I wanted to experience it all.

Later, when asked why he chose me out of all those girls, my husband answered, with a twinkle in his eye, "Simply good employee relations." As I see it, we met by chance. My husband thinks there's a bit more mystery to it, that it was fate. Either way, that day changed my life. Together Reinhard and I have built a happy marriage and a lifelong partnership. He is my life's love, together, hand in hand, forever.

2. A Woman's Life

I had to grow up quickly.

I was twenty-three when Brigitte, our first child, was born. Two years later Christoph arrived, and then Andreas. At twenty-eight I was already a mother of three small children, and I wanted to have a fourth. Unfortunately I couldn't, as I had suffered from acute kidney failure after my last pregnancy. After that, we even considered adopting, because I'd always thought it would be nice to have a lot of children. After all, that's what I was used to from my own family.

When you are young you don't think much about giving your life a specific direction. Unconsciously you simply follow the traditions and directions set by your parents. For me and my generation that meant raising families. And so, naturally, I thought children were an essential part of a complete life. To me that was just a matter of course.

I know now from experience that children enrich and shape our lives immeasurably. Today, couples can decide for themselves whether they want to have children or not. Personally, I think it's sad when a woman doesn't want to or can't have children, because I feel that without children a woman misses out on so many facets of life. A mother's love doesn't appear like magic when a child is born. On the contrary, it has to develop and grow. That kind of love, the love of a mother, is selfless. A mother loves and cares for her helpless child not to get something in return, but rather to protect, cherish, and help her child. She wants to do everything in her power to help her child become a good person. The gifts a mother treasures most are not material: a smile, a hug, an emotional bond, her child's trust. Those are the priceless rewards that make a mother happy.

I wish every woman could have the chance to experience this. A woman continues to grow through her children; they become her mirror. They stretch her character every single day, and they keep her on her toes at all times. A mother must try to be a role model at every moment, and in this way, a mother grows as a person. I wouldn't miss such an experience for anything—a mother's unparalleled opportunity to continuously grow and mature.

In his book, *The Art of Loving,* Erich Fromm comments on a mother's love: ". . . the relationship of mother and child is by its very nature one of inequality, where one needs all the help, and the other gives it. It is for this altruistic, unselfish character that motherly love has been considered the highest kind of love, and the most sacred of all emotional bonds."

Every single child is unique, and so is every single mother. In her heart she knows answers that cannot be found in any book. She wonders what makes a good mother, and whether she herself has been one. In my own case, my children are the only ones who could answer this question, but there nonetheless are a few signs that let me know that I have done a good job. My children still want to be close to me, they ask me for my advice, and they visit me regularly. We trust each other. Even though we may have the occasional difference of opinion, we are still a united family. This fills me with happiness and satisfaction.

In my life I have seen many different parts of the world, and I have experienced many different cultures and religions. I've seen that the common ground of all religions is that it is human to seek comfort and support for our beliefs, and I'm happy for those who can believe. But personally, I can't, because I'm rather skeptical. As a mother, I do know that if indeed there is life after death, it is through our children. We will continue to live through them long after our physical death. We will live on in their memories, their conversations, and their thoughts. We will live on in the genes we have passed on.

"He who lives in the memory of his loved ones is not dead. He is only removed. Death befalls only those who are forgotten." Those are the words of the great German philosopher Immanuel Kant. They express exactly how I feel and what I think.

Among all the responsibilities I've had in my life, my husband and my children have always been my first priority. Now my children are all grown up, living their own lives. In fact, two of them work in our company. The youngest one studied law and business. I am grateful for every minute I can be with them. When I get to see these young people, when they get off a plane, for example, and come toward me on the runway, tears well up in my eyes. That's how touched—and happy and proud of them—I am.

I had a full life as a young mother. I never imagined pursuing a career of my own. I lived a typical woman's life. When the children were small, I had girlfriends who also had small children. We would get together often to chat and spend time with each other. My sister and her two children would come over every day as well, so there was always a lot of life and commotion in our house.

Whenever he could, my husband would try to be home by bed-time. We called that special time "the kid's hour." He would play with them or tell them stories. He is a very good storyteller, and he enjoyed simply being with them. For someone who had never seen this firsthand it might be hard to believe, but even when the children came to his office for a visit, my husband would drop everything, take them on his lap, and make up stories. It was a special treat when he would make paper airplanes for them. He'd let them fly over the landing all the way down into the foyer of our company's building.

Trials and Tribulations

We had a heavy burden to carry. Our daughter Brigitte—we always called her Gitte—was very ill. She had asthma, and her first attack came when she was only four months old. Since then, I can't even count the times I've been in hospitals with her, full of trepidation, or the countless times I've held vigil at her bedside. She would have pneumonia as many as six times a year. She spent two years in clinics and hospitals, missing day after day of school. Until she turned twelve, I had many sleepless nights. I nearly reached the limits of my strength and energy. In those years, our entire family suffered.

We traveled to southern countries a lot, because the southern climate was helpful to her, and there Gitte and I would sleep on the beach so she could breathe more easily. I remember one trip in particular to the Grand Canaries when Gitte was seven years old. One day I noticed that her fingernails were black. What was happening to my child? A doctor told me later that it was the cortisone Gitte had to take that turned her nails black.

When we got back home, Gitte fell ill with pneumonia. There she was, my little girl, lying in bed, eyes closed, lips blue. She had a high fever and severe trouble breathing. I spent hours at her side, wrapping cold towels around her ankles, caressing her hot forehead, holding her hand, giving her water. But the fever just wouldn't subside. I was desperate. Why did she have to suffer so much? Panic and fear took hold of me. Was I going to lose her? I looked at her strained, pale face, almost transparent. I felt so helpless and lonely in these hours, but I held on to the memory of the joy and admiration I felt when I held her in my arms for the very first time. An eternity had passed since then. No, I wouldn't allow her to die. I would fight—fight for her, for all of us.

As I look back, I see that this was one of my moments of unimagined strength. I felt enormous power and conviction when I finally thought of my mother's household remedy. I took my feverish child and put her in the bathtub. I filled the tub with hot water, as hot as she could take it, and added mustard seeds. After I took her out of this bath, I poured ice cold water over her. The shock made her scream terribly, just as she was supposed to do. Screaming was part of the therapy, and it didn't bother me. I wanted her to survive, and that was all that mattered. I was absolutely convinced that she would make it. I wrapped her in cotton sheets and a blanket made of camel hair to make her sweat. I brought her back to bed and held her hand for hours, letting go only to wipe the sweat off her forehead or to change her damp sheets. Slowly her breathing calmed, and her lips began to turn rosy again. Four hours later the fever had gone down; she had made it through the crisis.

I'll never forget this experience. Later the doctors told me that she was very lucky, that only a very strong child should ever be put into a hot bathtub during a fever. Yet at the decisive moment my intuition had told me that it was the right thing to do. I had been absolutely convinced then, and it's during these rare moments that your conviction gives you the strength to do the right thing. Fate was on my side, and in the end, Gitte survived.

In all those years of her illness, we were fighting side by side. Gitte was a wonderful child. When I was desperate, she would smile at me, showing me her strong will to live. Yet she also had a delicate beauty that touched me. We gave each other courage. Sometimes all it took was a look into each other's eyes or a touch of the other's hand and we would both know that she'd beat this illness. It was during those times of hardship that I realized how very strong the bond between a mother and a daughter can be.

It was also during these times of hardship that I came to realize that one's mental strength can be passed onto others. I've seen that mysterious bond of souls in stroke victims as well. It's as if an energy moves among people in waves. Simple care can give so much comfort; emotional support can give so much help. The power of love born of compassion speeds up the healing process. Studies today confirm what I've intuitively known ever since I was a young mother. One study, conducted by Duke University, revealed that the oxygen supply of heart patients was better when a prayer was said in their presence. This proves it. No matter whether you say a prayer for a patient to give him strength and optimism, or whether you simply hold his hand, care in any shape or form strengthens the soul and assists in healing. To this day I believe that body and soul are one.

The experience of Gitte's illness had an immense effect on my personal growth. I began to question God, to wonder how He could allow such suffering in a small child. During the many trips I made to the hospital I saw so many other children suffering, children with leukemia who were doomed to die, children that made me feel so sad and helpless. Doubt crept into the beliefs I'd held since childhood. I began to doubt the existence of God, and to this day it is hard for me to believe in God's power and mercy. War, torture, and all the suffering in the world around us fan these doubts.

Even though this experience was so hard, there was a positive side to it as well. I realized that I had the strength and ability to make my own decisions. I had the power to do something, I was able to act quickly, and my efforts were successful. I got my daughter through this, and today she is a productive and cheerful young woman, something for which I will always be grateful.

My daughter and I are still very close. In many ways our relationship is like my relationship with my mother. We've talked on the telephone every day since she left Gütersloh, and even when we're thousands of miles apart she knows how I'm doing, simply by the sound of my voice.

Of course, I know from friends and acquaintances that some mother/daughter relationships are complicated and difficult, because they are defined by competition. I don't think this is true for us. That doesn't mean we don't argue once in a while.

Looking back, I remember another episode that gave me quite a scare. Our son Chris (whom we always called "Muscha"[1] as a child, because his short, bristly blond hair reminded us of a small kitten) had seen Brigitte take lots of medication. He must have been jealous of her, because he didn't need any medication himself. One afternoon both of them came staggering out of the children's room. I noticed that they had raided the medicine cabinet, and I knew they must have taken something. Well, I've never packed them up as quickly as I did then. I ran red lights to get them to Professor Müller, who knew Gitte very well, at the chil-

[1] *Muschi* is a colloquial German term for "kitten."

dren's hospital in Bethel. I was so worried that they had poisoned themselves. Both had their stomachs pumped immediately. Once again I found myself in the hospital, and once again I was lucky. They were just fine.

A Good Upbringing

The way I wanted to raise my children was shaped greatly by my experiences in the Pathfinders. Honesty, decency, and fairness were the values I wanted to pass on. Even when my children were small I would always say: Honesty is the best policy, even if it's difficult. Avoid lies and secrecy. Be friendly to other people. Give gifts, no matter how small, and make them yourself. Our children plucked countless flowers and drew numerous pictures to give to our friends and coworkers as presents, something I've always supported. And finally, I also passed on the Pathfinder motto: Don't let a day go by without doing a good deed.

I didn't want my children to become arrogant. I wanted them to treat people with respect, no matter what their roles in life. I always say, "Everyone is a piece of the puzzle in our society." Our family has always been down-to-earth, and we never considered living the superficial life of the jet set. Work and a sense of duty have always been a part of our lives. But our lives weren't a bed of roses, either. Illness and worries have visited us, just like anybody, because money and professional success cannot protect you from that. Our family has always remained humble and grateful. Put simply, you don't develop character if you've never cried. My children experienced life in all its different facets. They've experienced joy and beauty, but they've also experienced worry and suffering. In short, we are a very normal family.

So many people, many of them children, don't have a roof over their heads or a warm bed to sleep in or enough to eat. So many people experience war, live as refugees, or suffer injuries and terrible diseases. So many people are born into miserable circumstances through no fault of their own. So many children have no opportunities because they never learned how to read and write, because they never get the chance to develop their talents, or because they have to fight for simple survival day in and day out. Again and again I would tell my children how comfortable their Western European lives were. I wanted them to be grateful for waking up in clean white sheets every morning. I wanted them to appreciate their warm rooms and our tables full of food. I wanted them to cherish their schooling and the opportunity to learn. And I wanted them to treasure the love and protection their parents offered them. My hope was that they would appreciate our privileged life, and not take anything for granted.

The financial support that we gave them when they were students was hardly substantial, and they weren't exactly able to live it up. We wanted them to experience what it means to get by on a shoestring. They didn't own expensive cars, and they lived in simple apartments. It was always important to us to prepare our children for real life, to teach them to live independently and responsibly. We wanted them to make their own way. We felt that humility was the virtue necessary to accomplish that.

I had my children excused from all classes on the sacrament of confession. I didn't want them to have to go to confession at the age of nine. I believe that there is no need to create a sense of guilt at a time when most likely they haven't yet done anything wrong. As an adult this seemed like brainwashing to me. What is a nine-year-old supposed to confess? They haven't committed any sins yet. And what exactly is sin anyway? Is it a sin when they snatch an eraser, or sneak in a piece of chocolate before dinner, or touch themselves? Some children make up sins just to have something to confess, which to me that seems like actually teaching them how to cheat and lie. I didn't want that for my children. I had no intention of exposing them to dogma, either. I did want them to learn the principles of Christianity, albeit without confession, and after a bit of convincing our priest complied.

I'm not against religion. On the contrary. Humans are not perfect, and I believe that we need an ethical foundation to provide our lives with direction. If religion is benevolent, it can provide us with meaning for our lives and our deaths. Religion can provide a spiritual home and the promise of transcendence. I support that because I believe, simply, to each their own.

Yet I myself have trouble with many dogmas of the church. One of them is the Catholic idea of confession. Another is the way sexuality is dealt with. It seems like the church's view of sexuality is based on fear. These old structures need to be broken and adapted to our times. If only the churches were able to give more practical assistance to people in need, if only sermons were closer to the issues of real life and real people, religion could offer a haven to many souls in need, and I'm sure the churches would fill up again[2].

I believe in the power of love. Christian love, understanding, and forgiveness can lead the way to true humanity. It is so easy to give love, because love is friendly, kind, and comforting. Love lends an open ear and cares. Love is the comfort that lights up our lives. It bestows sight and insight, and it respects boundaries. Love generously offers help and comfort without ulterior motives. It overcomes borders and limits and instead creates closeness and trust. Love, and love alone, makes our lives unique and gives us meaning. Without meaning, life is empty. Without love, our spirit will never be satisfied and will be forever restless.

Long ago I decided to take the road of love and compassion. In addition to Christian ethics, I have studied the moral teachings of Confucius, one of China's great sages. What attracts me to his philosophy is that it deals with real people and practical life. As in Christianity, the guiding principle for behavior is the golden rule: "Do unto others as you would have them do unto you." I am strongly drawn to the ideals of a refined character, self-control, politeness, consideration for others, and moderation in thought and action. He who is honorable will answer kindness with kindness, and evil with justice. The ideal is to allow individuals, families, and governments to find a basis in the spirit of humanity. This can be achieved by following the five cardinal virtues: re-

[2] In Germany, churches are losing support, and going to Mass is not in style.

ciprocal love, honesty, wisdom, morality, and sincerity. If everyone sincerely strives for self-improvement, we all will benefit. Governments will work well, and those in charge will be role models.

Whether it is the Ten Commandments of Christianity or the ethics of Confucius that provide structure to our lives, I think that just a fraction of these ideals of moral behavior, if put into action, would help to overcome the increasing egotism in Western society. We need to come together and learn once again how to live as a community.

If we were to give one another more respect, more compassion, and more attention, the lives in our families, in our states, in our entire society could improve. It is the spirit of humanity that holds a society together. Without the spirit of humanity our civilization couldn't survive, and we would succumb to barbarism.

Being a Role Model and Setting Limits

Despite my unaffected and cheerful nature, I was rather self-conscious when I was young. I needed to exercise all my will-power to move among groups of people I didn't know. When I visited my husband in his office on Friday nights, for example, when he was with colleagues sipping a glass of wine, my heart would pound in my chest. I was just that insecure in these situations. It took a lot of training and inner growth to learn to step beyond my trepidaton and approach other people with more confidence. I had to work hard on myself, so once again my stamina came in very handy. Again and again I tried to approach strangers and strike up a conversation. I reminded myself that I'd need to be courageous enough to make mistakes. I'd think: Remember, nobody is perfect. Better luck next time. There's always a second chance. That's what I say. I've always been a fighter.

I was a real fighter, and today I am able to connect with all kinds of people, no matter what their background or social status might be. I am able to talk to members of the board of directors as easily as to doormen, to queens as to clerks, to presidents as to professors. Remembering my earlier insecurities helps me to make these connections. I know how grateful people are when they are met with friendliness. That's how to create human closeness. This is so clear to me when I visit stroke victims, or when I participate in self-help groups. It's also apparent in my day-to-day relationships with coworkers on any of my numerous projects. It is compassion that allows me to get that close. It's genetic . . . my mother's legacy, so to speak. Actually, I think that my compassion was mostly honed by watching my mother's example.

The importance of compassion and empathy in daily life is excellently described in the book *Emotional Intelligence* by the American psychologist Daniel Goleman. He claims that our psychological connection to others, upon which our entire emotional life is based, depends on our ability to recognize and interpret other people's emotions. He argues that this ability can be applied successfully to such diverse areas as sales and management, love and childrearing, caretaking of others, and even political activities. The inability to read other people's emotions, on the other hand, is what Goleman calls a lack of emotional intelligence and an immense deficit of humanity. He explains that understanding other people's emotions requires interpretation of nonverbal signs such as a certain tone of voice, facial expression, posture, and the telltale sign of trembling hands. This in turn requires sensitivity and empathy. How right he is. If you are able to discern what other people feel, approaching them is much easier and more satisfying at the same time.

I didn't want my children to ever experience my insecurities. Many young people are so shy and insecure, especially during adolescence. I made it a point early on to involve my children when we had guests. They helped set the table, they greeted the guests, they took pictures. Sometimes they even chauffeured them around. After dinner, when my son would ask, "Mr. von

Karajan[3], may I take a picture of you?" he wasn't turned down. What a moment of success for him. Or my other son, while driving an important guest to the hotel, couldn't just sit at the wheel, mute as a fish. No, he would have to chat. Thus, in a rather natural way, my children learned not to be afraid of celebrities and important people. When we would travel to foreign countries, we would sometimes have our children run errands, so that they would have to deal with the foreign currency and the foreign language.

We raised our children with love and understanding, yet we also set limits. When at fifteen our daughter wanted to have a moped, we clearly said no. We just thought it was too dangerous, because we had heard so much about accidents involving mopeds. A targeted "no" is very important for a child's education. Of course, it is much easier to say "yes." "No" takes a lot of patience, as I know from experience. But sometimes it is a "no" rather than a "yes" that shows that you love and care about your child.

We had many discussions and arguments in our home. Sometimes, when there was no end to an argument in sight, I would finish it right then and there. Enough is enough. Children don't have an adult's experiences and therefore may not yet be able to accept the voice of reason. Therefore parents shouldn't allow themselves to be pulled into long and drawn-out arguments with their children. For what begins as a calm discussion may end in a nasty fight.

When our children were stubborn and would scream, they'd first meet with a wet washcloth. The shock would stop their tantrums immediately. That's how our parents handled us, and that's how I handled my children. I would still do this today. It is a very effective method to make children listen to the voice of reason. It doesn't hurt and won't injure the soul. Yet if I had known then what I know now about childhood development, I would have been more patient. I would have explained more. I

[3] Herbert von Karajan is one of the most renowned conductors in Europe. He has toured the world with the Berlin Philharmonic.

would have held them in my arms and said: "There's no need to cry . . . I understand why you are sad."

As a parent you are bound to make mistakes. I'm sure I did. Naturally I feel bad about that today, but parenting is an acquired skill. Therefore, when your children are older, sit down, talk to them, and admit to your mistakes. It's important. Nobody is perfect—not even parents. That is one very important lesson they will learn from you. And bear in mind that accepting one's mistakes, being able to recognize them and admit to them, is a lesson we all should remember. After all, parents are supposed to be role models.

All children should not be treated the same. Every child has his or her own personality. One may need to be encouraged, whereas the other may need to be cautioned. They may have different talents, too. One may be artistically inclined, whereas the other may be more intellectual. Parents need to acknowledge that, and should always nourish the specific talents their children have. Our children, for example, were all pretty good at drawing, so I had them take lessons with an artist. They were so enthusiastic! They could be creative and make something themselves, and they enjoyed it a great deal. These moments of success gave them great satisfaction and provided them with a center. I hung their "works" in the kitchen, in the dining room, and in the bedroom. I still have them to this day. As another example, our son Christoph put together a toy race track by himself without ever having read the instructions. He has always had an exceptional talent for technical things, and we have always made sure to encourage that. And finally, my children even had good business sense. When they would collect cowslips in the woods, they'd open up shop along the road and sell them. They'd come home with their profits, beaming with pride.

It is vital that parents respect a child's personality rather than try to shape him or her based on their own expectations. I know how hard this can be for parents, and watching young mothers today, I feel that many of them are not quite up to the task. Looking back, I don't think I was quite ready yet, either. But isn't it true that no task is more important than that of safely guiding a child through our increasingly complicated society? Our future depends on our children.

On a daily basis we hear horror stories about the increasing crime rate among young people, along with the growing use of violence during conflicts. One of the many reasons I see for such behavior is the moral neglect and lovelessness of a free-spirited upbringing which neither sets sufficient limits nor provides any ideals. Children suffer from such a lack of care and comfort.

Many parents are overwhelmed by the need to multitask in a fast-paced world. They are insecure, and may not know where to set limits and where to give in. It seems as if we've lost our natural instincts that tell us how to raise our offspring. We need to see children with our hearts to know what's right, because in the end, raising children is an art. It is the art of setting clear limits while still nurturing their strengths and abilities. Raising children means providing guidance, assistance, and support on their way toward independence, so that they may be able to cope on their own. This takes time. It takes patience and strength. And above all, it takes love, warmth, and sensitivity. Some parents don't have these qualities. Still others don't want to make the effort. Raising children takes someone who has a sense of inner security, someone who has a goal in mind for rasing his or her children.

Our Western culture is based on respect for the human spirit. It is based on the Christian principles of love and tolerance. Our culture depends on a sense of responsibility for the community. It depends on the acceptance of law and order, but our nuclear families place less and less importance on the value of role models. The truth is that today's absentee parents cannot be role models. The problem is that it is easier and more motivating to learn by imitation rather than from dry principles. Children take in moral knowledge by imitating role models. Children need someone to relate to, and they need people to care for them. Unfortunately, many parents are under so much stress that they have neither the patience nor the energy to deal with their offspring after a day's work. Our families and our neighborhoods no longer provide a tightly-knit social net; more and more of society's structures are breaking apart. And to make matters worse, some parents care less about their children because they have become egotistical, and place their own interests above those of their children.

Then there is the lack of manners, beginning with a lack of "please" and "thank you," and ending with inconsiderate and self-important behavior. It should be praised openly if a young person offers his seat to an elderly person, or holds the door for someone else. This type of politeness shows respect for elders, but unfortunately it is rare these days. I think that's regrettable. Many teachers complain that they have to make up at school for what parents fail to teach at home, but our schools are not equipped to handle that kind of responsibility. Social behavior and good manners are a barometer for the conditions of any culture and society.

Historically, the extended family was able to provide comfort and safety. When the parents were unavailable, siblings, grandparents, aunts, uncles, cousins, or other family members took care of the children. The children were never left to their own devices. Unfortunately, lonely children are the norm in our nuclear families or in the single-parent households so typical of today. What we lose is a sense of community and the ability to relate to one another. The process of individualization, a disastrous process, continues. What is at its end? A society of disturbed and frightened people? Who will catch us when we fall? Who will hold our hands when we are in need?

We must rekindle our sense of community, and teach once more the principles of the common good in schools and homes. A democracy geared towards the participation and autonomy of the individual depends on our ability to deal with conflict and make compromises.

A Sense of Community

In our present society nobody seems to want to talk about the principle of the common good, let alone try to live it. This is partially due to a planned and desired change of direction in our educational system, which presently favors a misunderstood goal of individual self-realization. A sense of community is rarely part of the curriculum. From what I hear from friends and coworkers with school-aged children, it is virtually impossible these days to develop a sense of togetherness at school. Competition is so great that students no longer help one another with their schoolwork. During tests, for example, students no longer allow their classmates to copy from one another anymore. On the contrary, they apparently build walls around their papers to make copying during tests virtually impossible. Not that I'm in favor of cheating, of course, but the attitude of the lonesome rider seems to me to indicate that the camaraderie we once practiced in school no longer exists. Everybody fights against everybody else in the competition for the good grades that will open the door to the right colleges and universities.

In a roundtable discussion, twenty experts and I discussed the topic of education at length. We asked the following question: How can we develop a sense of community among our children? We all came to the same conclusion: Solidarity is indeed the most important lesson our society has to re-learn. Every single citizen must know how important solidarity is. Its lack is apparent everywhere: in increasingly inconsiderate or even criminal behavior, in the constant elbowing for space, and in a growing egotism coupled with a lack of social commitment. Only a long and arduous process will bring about a turnarond of our ideals from our extreme individualization back to a sense of commitment to others. Our present condition does not seem to allow us to exhibit any solidarity at all. This worries me greatly. We have to re-learn a sense of community, solidarity, and togetherness in order to meet the challenges of the future, but I ask myself: Will future generations be able to turn things around?

Our children need a spiritual direction. The sixties dismantled authority, broke with old and traditional structures, and brought new freedom. And in the years since, we have realized that this freedom requires responsibility. The freedom of the individual ends when it infringes upon the rights of others. This means simply that children need limits. We should have a continuous dialogue about the need for limits without fear of being stigmatized with the label of authoritarianism. Our educational principles need to develop and change when times develop and change.

Children want and need to be challenged. A good education should assist every young person in setting goals that, on the one hand, cater to individual talents and professional ideals while, on the other hand, also contribute to the common good. Our schools should support our children in this by arranging and encouraging practical training in business and civics.

Punishment is justified if it keeps a child from developing in the wrong direction. By punishment I mean a set of restrictions or the kind of additional work that will make children and young people think. Our duty as adults is to protect our children, and sometimes this may include protecting them from themselves. I remember how two of my children set fire to a wastepaper basket in a hotel. Just like other kids their age (they were five and seven years old) they were a bit wild, as can be the case in all families. This is the only time my husband resorted to corporal punishment, and I still feel he was justified. He had no other choice than to send a clear message.

Punishment requires consistency, which is sometimes inconvenient. A young couple recently told me that they grounded their ten-year-old boy on a Saturday because he had done something wrong. Only after they had imposed this punishment did they realize that they had arranged to meet with friends to play tennis that afternoon. In order to be consistent and supervise their boy's enforced stay at home, they had to cancel. Raising children takes an effort. It is inconvenient, because it makes demands on your own needs. Many young parents are not prepared to accept that.

But always remember, even if there are problems, parents should always provide their children with warmth and comfort. Holding them in your arms, explaining things, and talking to them may get the desired results more effectively than yet another reprimand.

As I came to realize all of these issues of parenting, I thought that "Parenting" should be a mandatory class in school. It would help to prepare young people for their role as fathers and mothers, and teach them how to deal with conflict situations. Incidentally, England is actually experimenting with parenting classes in its schools. I'm curious to see the results. Perhaps we will all profit from this.

Communication

During my time as a stay-at-home mother and homemaker I grew immensely, matured, and learned. My husband was my teacher. My family background, along with my father's fate, had made it impossible for me to go to college. But my husband gave me the once-in-a-lifetime opportunity to make up for that. My dialogue with him replaced the schooling, the practical training, and the lectures I had missed out on. I learned and learned and learned. . . .

He told me how he had started his business, and how he would solve company problems. I listened. He discussed politics, government, and society. He shared his opinions and critically analyzed everything. Again I listened. He spoke of ethics and morality. Still I listened. Never once was he condescending. On the contrary, when I had a question, he would patiently explain. This is also how he handled our children. He passed on an incredible wealth of knowledge and experience. Like a sponge, I absorbed everything I could during these years. I learned critical thinking, and how to question and analyze.

He also taught me how to listen to my body. He led a simple, virtually ascetic life. He exercised regularly, and ate and drank in moderation. So I began to live more conscientiously as well. I began to exercise, too. He claimed that the "virtue of moderation" was the most valuable insight he had gained from his Greek lessons. Plato's and Aristotle's ethics teach that it is through balance and moderation alone that we will achieve personal happiness and harmony. My husband followed this principle with amazing discipline, and he passed it on to me. Being with him has been a continuous process of growth and learning.

Of course, he dominated our relationship, but even though he is twenty years my senior, he learned something from me, too. We were complete opposites: He was a well-rounded personality, a thinker, a philosopher; I, on the other hand, was young, carefree, and merry. After all, I had just stepped out from under my mother's wings. He had already started a business, and had been to war as a young soldier. The men in his generation had been through so much in their young lives. I, on the other hand, was full of dreams.

I have always been a "people person," so I loved having many friends around. But my husband wasn't used to that, so I brought him together with new people. When we went on vacation to Rhodes, for example, we would take walks on the private beach belonging to Anthony Quinn. In the beginning we were by ourselves, but after a short while we would be surrounded by a group of merry people. We loved it. On future trips more and more of our friends and relatives would come with us. Often we would be up to fifteen or twenty people spending carefree days together, sipping a glass of good wine. We would sing Pathfinder songs that I taught them. This gave my husband, who enjoyed singing as well, a chance to impress everyone with his wonderful voice. I told him many times that he could have been a recording star had his life taken a different turn. We spent many fun vacation days with groups of friends.

I've always claimed that I am the butterfly in my husband's life. As I said, we are different in many respects, yet in others, we are very similar. We are both athletic, and we both love nature and enjoy its intense beauty. Still, sometimes it is difficult to blend our differences. This causes many couples to grow apart and give up. They are not willing to accept nor tolerate each other's differences. But I think it's great if you can see your partner as a welcome addition to your life, if you can see that he or she brings to the relationship some characteristics you do not have. Looking at it from this point of view, you will notice that differences in personality enrich a partnership rather than burden it. Obviously this doesn't work without a healthy dose of tolerance and generosity. If a partnership works despite the partners' differences, it is one of the most beautiful things you will ever share with another person. As for my husband and I, I believe that we are doing a pretty good job. We have been a good team for a long time, and we are grateful for that.

Again, my husband was once in the army, and anyone who has been though such an experience has trouble expressing his emotions, trouble trusting and giving love. It is not easy to learn how to talk about emotions. But it is possible, if you have someone who takes you by the hand. I don't have any trouble at all showing my feelings. It is so easy for me to tell my husband and my children that I love them. I'm not afraid to get close, either. On the contrary, I enjoy a good hug, I like caressing people and holding their hands. It's my way of showing how close I feel to my family and friends, male and female alike.

A partnership requires a person to change and adapt constantly. Couples have to be considerate to each other, and look closely to see what the other one might need. For example, I had to learn to curb my impulses, and not to bombard my husband with petty issues in the evening after a hard day's work. I had to learn to be diplomatic and to wait for the right moment to bring up important matters.

I can remember one episode that illustrates how I put my newly acquired skill of diplomacy to work for me. It was on a trip to Argentina. My husband had important business meetings, and I wanted to do some shopping. My husband murmured absent-mindedly, "Why don't you buy yourself something?" There are beautiful antique shops in Buenos Aires, and I took a good look at every one of them. When I came home that evening without anything, my husband asked whether I hadn't seen anything I liked. I just shook my head. The next morning he gave me some jewelry that I still like wearing to this day. He thought I should have something to remind me of this trip. But then, six weeks later, back home in Gütersloh, my husband was rather surprised to see several antiques being unloaded in front of our house. I had bought them in Buenos Aires as a surprise for him. I think every wife can tell stories like that. Sometimes you just have to treat your partner with diplomacy.

While I had to learn to be quiet at the right moment, my husband had to learn to talk. He had to learn to say things like, "I can't right now, but later on I'd love to take some time for a conversation with you." Sometimes that's not easy. But to remain silent in these moments is a failure to show how you feel. That can be quite a strain on a relationship. Every married couple goes through their own individual process of learning about and adapting to each other.

"Learn how to talk so that others will hear you." I heard those words from a priest on the radio. How true. Children, partners, even friends have to learn how to talk to one another to avoid misunderstandings. Otherwise people will hurt one another unnecessarily by creating tension when things are left unsaid. You shouldn't withdraw in silence, because if people don't know what they've done wrong, they cannot change or improve.

I hear that many married couples talk to each other for an average of only four minutes. I feel sorry for these couples. My husband and I talk to each other all the time. We talk over a cup of coffee for about thirty minutes every morning, and, if possible, in the evening in front of the fireplace for about an hour or two over a glass of wine. Those are our rituals. We talk about what happened that day, as well as our thoughts and opinions regarding events in the company. We also discuss current economic, social, and political issues. We both adhere to an unspoken rule: The mornings are reserved for difficult topics, whereas the evenings are reserved for pleasant or neutral things. This recipe works to avoid sleepless nights.

When we're on vacation, of course, we have all day to talk to each other. We don't listen to music or watch TV, because we have so much to say to each other. We never run out of things to talk about. We chat about people close to us. We discuss religion, different cultures, or politics. We talk about our childhood and our family. We share all our experiences, and talk about absolutely everything that is important to us. And we even write to each other often. My husband diligently collected forty-eight folders full of letters and notes we wrote to each other over the course of time. Sometimes, when I come home after a trip, I'll find a note from my husband on the grand piano saying, "I can't wait to see you!" Or when I come home late after an event and I won't see him because he's already in bed, he writes, "Thinking of you." Sometimes I get a rhymed fax. My husband is rather talented at rhyming. He really enjoys it! Friends, acquaintances, assistants, and household help have received rhyming notes and messages. And the beautiful letters he writes! On birthdays, at Christmas, and at the New Year we write to each other. It is so nice to think about your partner in that way. I am always happy when I hear my husband say, "I want to be with my wife until she turns eighty." That will make him one hundred. We will do what we can to make that work out.

An Important Decision

I've mentioned before that there have been turning points in my life, moments when sudden clarity came over me. Often you carry things around with you, unconsciously, without noticing them. And then suddenly, thoughts or feelings that have been foggy surface and become crystal clear. What triggers them is usually of minor importance. Your partner may have moved a certain way, or he may have used a certain tone of voice, or his body language caught your eye. Something makes us see each other in a new and different light. Sometimes what seems like distance helps us see things more clearly and allows us to draw new conclusions.

I had one of these moments on a certain morning twenty-three years ago. This morning was to change my life completely. I remember it as if it were yesterday. My husband was sitting next to me. We were having coffee together. The house was empty, and we were alone with each other, because our youngest child had just started school a few weeks earlier. My husband was telling me what he was working on in the company. It was a very typical situation for many young couples at the time. The husband talks about his work, the wife listens.

That morning, however, I wasn't able to be "all ears." It was as if my husband had disappeared behind a cloud of fog. His voice seemed to come from far away, and for the first time I noticed that we were living in two completely separate worlds. I was telling him about my life at home with the children, whereas he was telling me about his life at work. What I saw was a chasm between us.

When he left for work that day I felt empty. I realized that I had to do something about this situation. With my children away at school and the household in the able hands of our housekeeper, I had a lot of spare time to make use of. I didn't want to play bridge or golf or tennis. I didn't want to spend my time as an adornment at numerous parties. I wanted to do something worthwhile, so I came to a conclusion. I would go to work. I wanted to be productive, to show him that I could make my way in the professional world as well. I wanted to get to know my husband's world. Our company was his life, and I wanted to partake of it with him.

I remembered what I had heard and read about his grandmother, Friedericke Bertelsmann. She died in 1946 at the age of eighty-seven. She was the last person born with the Bertelsmann name. She was a rather strong woman with a healthy sense of community. She brought sandwiches and coffee to the shift workers herself when they were working overtime. Religion and church played a major role in her life. When, during the Christmas season, Bertelsmann books were sold out and had to be reprinted, the managers would let the printing machines run seven days a week. Yet on Sundays, Friedericke Bertelsmann would simply press a button and turn them off. It was her opinion that nobody should have to work on Sunday. In her representative role in the business, she took care of social issues. Her personality was a model for me. I didn't have to work for a living, so I was able to use my time and energy in the service of others.

Later I told my husband about my idea of going to work. He reacted more positively than I had imagined. All he said was, "Why not give it a try?" Since I know him well, it was clear to me that this is how he was showing his full support.

3. First Forays into the
Professional World

My first forays into the professional world had a lot to do with my personal situation. My intuition told me that, just like me, the wives of the Bertelsmann managers might have very little knowledge of the professional lives of their husbands. I wanted to do something to counter that, because I find it problematic when wives don't know anything about their husbands' professional lives. Many men spend more time in the office than at home with their families. They work with people their wives may never have even met. If a wife is not interested in her husband's profession, a very important part of her husband's life will remain a secret to her, because many men don't talk much about their work. That's dangerous to a relationship, because husband and wife may grow apart.

My idea was to put together regular events that would allow the wives to learn something about their husbands' work. Every event started with a lecture given by a manager of our publishing house, and ended with a dinner afterwards which allowed us to chat and get to know each other. It all started with a group of just forty women. They were enthusiastic that I had opened doors with this idea. They were all grateful that I had taken the initiative.

To this day, our group of "Bertelswomen" still exists. Our numbers have grown to about 140. This initiative has established long-lasting contacts, and even some friendships. For quite some time we've been taking annual trips together, and I always make sure that our trips have an interesting agenda.

For example, in 1998 we flew to Nepal and India. In Katmandu in Nepal, and in New Delhi and Agra in India we experienced two very different cultures. A well-informed tour guide from India explained everything to us. We visited a Buddhist cloister in Nepal, drove in bicycle rickshaws through the old part of New Delhi, dined in the German embassy, and visited a few temples, including the shrine built where Mahatma Gandhi was cremated. This place touched me immensely. With nonviolent resistance, Gandhi showed how powerful people can be with strength of will alone. He became a role model to the entire world, myself included. Armed with nothing but the truth, he made his opponents acknowledge their mistakes and thus change their ways. His attitude and his civil courage prevented great bloodshed during the Indian Independence Movement. There are not many people with that much inner strength.

At a dinner at the German embassy in New Delhi I heard about Sister Lilly, a nun who took care of Indian orphans. I made a spontaneous appointment to visit the orphanage the next day. All of the women in my group were very moved by the difficult conditions Sister Lilly had to deal with in her work. The children were missing everything, especially clothes. So, back in Gütersloh, we all collected clothing for the children and sent them to India. We also collected money for the orphanage. We still write to Sister Lilly regularly, and she tells us how she fights for "her" children.

In 1999 we did something very special. We flew to Japan to see the gala concert given during the Asian part of our international singing contest, New Voices. About 150 young Asian vocal artists took part in this competition. The event took place in a theater in Yokusaka, Japan. Yokusaka, a town of approximately four hundred thousand inhabitants, is about one hour from Tokyo by train. In front of an audience of about eighteen hundred I gave a speech that touched upon the sad history our two countries have in common. Both our countries experienced a devastating period of war, after which we both were able to work toward an enormous economic boom. Now, fortunately, both countries still enjoy a long-standing period of peace. Yet numerous Japanese and German mothers and wives lost their sons and their husbands. The experience of such hardship overcomes cultural barriers. The Japanese were moved. After my speech, there was a moment of silence, before the audience burst into thunderous applause. I felt then that I had touched their hearts.

The meeting of the two cultures was extremely interesting. On our second day, unfortunately, it rained constantly. It was a storm, almost like a typhoon. Umbrellas would break apart or fly away. Even so, our hosts never wore coats. I didn't understand that until somebody told me that the Japanese code of behavior considers wearing a coat impolite towards guests. I can still remember the men out there in the pouring rain, pants wet, jackets soaked, because the small women's umbrellas just wouldn't keep them dry. I told them how sorry I was that they were getting so wet. Polite as always, the Japanese just smiled and said that they were sorry that we had to experience such bad weather during our visit.

The next day the women were able to take a very short tour of Tokyo and the Emperor's town of Kyoto. Then we had to fly back to Germany. It was a short but very interesting five-day tour. We saw and learned quite a bit.

Since then our women's circle has become firmly established in our company. Whenever a fundraiser is necessary, the women are right there. They make presents by hand, make marmalade, bake cookies, and sell handmade lace work and silk paintings at our annul Christmas bazaar. The profit goes to our campaign to combat uveitis, an illness that afflicts the eyes, or to any of our other projects. Thirteen of the women volunteer for the German Stroke Foundation, which I founded in 1992. One of them, for example, Doris Lanninger, whose husband was a member of the upper management at Bertelsmann, has been volunteering two or three days a week in the office of the Foundation. She spends her time writing letters, preparing mailings, and answering the phones. One day, when her husband felt numb in one of his legs, she rushed him to the hospital. She knew that this could be the first sign of a stroke, and she was right. Her husband was fortunate because he received immediate help. This story shows how important it is to always remain open to new knowledge. Had Doris Lanninger not been interested in and committed to the Foundation, would she have known that her husband needed help so quickly? He might not be healthy enough to work today. She and her friend Anette Harnischfeger continue to lead one of our self-help groups.

Monika Abel is another woman who volunteers for the Bertelsmann Foundation, and supports the campaign against uveitis. She is a teacher, and her husband is in upper management at Bertelsmann. Mrs. Abel selects the topics and speakers for our events, she takes notes in the self-help groups, and she handles relations with those seeking advice. She even put together a weekend phone service for those who are afflicted with uveitis.

We particularly enjoyed the fashion bazaar we put together for the Bertelsmann employees. This was one of my spontaneous ideas during one of the regular meetings with the women. We were talking about a problem many women seem to have with their wardrobe: They claim to have nothing to wear, even though their closets are stuffed. As always, my instincts were to seek an immediate solution. When I suggested organizing a fashion sale, everyone was enthusiastic. We all went through our closets to find any spare clothing that we no longer wear. We also ordered spare merchandise from local textile factories. Shoes, handbags, and jewelry completed the sale. We staged a fashion show in the foyer of our Foundation, with some of us ladies presenting the most beautiful pieces. There was music, drinks were served, and then the sale began. We had a great time trying on one another's clothes and giving fashion advice. The atmosphere was terrific. We took in about 30,000 German marks (US $15,000) for the German Stroke Foundation.

My success with the ladies' group gave me the courage to look for other things to do. I started a "Bertelsmen for Bertelsmen" fund, which assists employees and their families experiencing unforeseen hardship. Every "Bertelsman" and "Bertelswoman" is encouraged to donate a few pennies from each paycheck for this initiative. Many of our employees donate the 20 German marks (US $10) they receive from the company for their birthday every year to this initiative as well. In addition, I had collection stands, shaped like red hearts installed in the company's main administration building, as well as in the Foundation offices. Every employee and every visitor can give money anonymously, and with this income we help people discreetly. For example, we were able to pay off a retired woman's debts that were amassed by her alcoholic husband. And we helped another woman with lodging so she could be close to her child, who was in the hospital. We helped a widow with three small children keep the family home after her husband had died of cancer, leaving behind a lot of debt. We helped to furnish the new home of one of our employees who had, along with her children, left her abusive husband. And finally we make sure that one of our employees, who had a cerebral infarction, sees his parents on a regular basis, because their visits will help the young man recover quickly. We pay their way to the rehabilitation center, since the parents, who live on a small pension, cannot afford the trip.

Last year the fund had an income of 12,000 German marks (US $6,000). Of course, the company could help, too. But I think it's particularly important that this "Bertelsmen and Bertelswomen helping one another" initiative exists, because it encourages the better-off employees to make small sacrifices, strengthening a sense of unity among the workforce.

Great Misfortune as My Teacher

My work was beginning to take more and more of my time. I felt like a student of this new world, and I behaved accordingly. I was careful to try and curb my spontaneity with diplomacy. But inside I was alert, eagerly searching for new responsibilities.

Looking back, I realized that my life had always been overshadowed by illness. Not only were my children sick a lot, but I myself suffered my share of illness. I had spent several months in the University Hospital in Münster, suffering from unexplained intestinal bleeding. At some point during my illness I overheard a physician saying, "She's got six weeks at the most." I'll never forget the shock I felt. But then my mother took me to the hospital, where an old nun realized that I had an intestinal fistula. I had surgery in the children's hospital in Bethel. They didn't put me on the children's floor, but in a room with several women, who made sure that I wouldn't have any water after the surgery, which would have been dangerous.

But it was four weeks after my third child, Andreas, was born that I went through the most severe health-related crisis of my life. I suffered from a life-threatening kidney failure. One of my kidneys had stopped working altogether, and the other one was barely functioning. My husband had found me in bed covered with rashes, a green tongue, and extremely painful colic. He rushed me to the hospital, where I had surgery, and where I remained for four weeks. By the time I left the hospital, I weighed a mere eighty-four pounds.

This incident brought home how it feels to be completely dependent on the assistance of others. I will never forget those moments, for they shaped my life. I experienced firsthand the gift of being helped. These life-threatening situations have shown me that there are no guarantees in life, and so I was able to remain humble despite my successes. Some people become egotistical and heartless once they're successful. They become blind towards other people's hardships, and won't give credit to anyone but themselves. I, on the other hand, have grown from the trials and tribulations fate has bestowed on me. I have become more accepting of other people's weaknesses, and more sensitive to their needs. My personal misfortunes have prevented me from wasting my life with the superficialities so many others engage in. I've always been deeply grateful for the good things in my life. It is this sense of gratitude that gives me strength in the service of the needy. I will never forget what it is like to live humbly, what it is like to not know much, what it is like to have limited opportunities in your life.

And whenever I needed help or advice with regard to my children in the years gone by, physicians, nurses, friends and acquaintances have always been there for me. So many have been willing to offer helpful advice, from the kind of medication to take to the best diet and the most effective natural remedies to follow. Many were deeply sympathetic with my anxieties, and readily offered compassion. I've always had the support and help I needed.

I've tried to never lose sight of the positive things in my life. I've been so very fortunate. Meeting my husband, whom I love very much, was one of the greatest gifts in my life. I'm so fortunate to be loved by him, for many women never get to experience love. He's always supported me in everything, whereas so many other men dominate their wives and keep them from being productive. I'm so fortunate to have children whom I was able to raise to be productive and energetic young people despite their many health issues. I'm so fortunate to be financially independent. So many people have to struggle for food every single day, fighting to make ends meet. All this has made me grateful rather than arrogant.

Through my husband I encountered Greek philosophy. Aristotle, for example, believed that man can only be happy if he is able to develop all of his abilities and make use of all of his opportunities. And my own experience teaches me the same thing. Without my husband I probably never would have realized all my talents. You can only find your talents if you challenge yourself, if you work. You have to test yourself and develop your creativity. A lack of challenge will make you unhappy.

I firmly believe that it is the responsibility of those who are strong to care for those who are weak. Those of us who have a lot to give can offer support to those who don't have enough for themselves. I have a lot of strength and time. I can and I want to help! I want to contribute to the common good. I consider this to be my social responsibility. It is practical and practiced solidarity.

The Bertelsmann Foundation

Founded by my husband in 1977, the Bertelsmann Foundation gave me the opportunity to act on my beliefs in the value of solidarity. My husband was convinced that our country didn't realize the immense implications of global competition. The Bertelsmann Foundation was founded to research and develop solutions for a wide range of society's social, political, and economic problems. The idea was to incorporate global information into a mix of research and hands-on development. The Foundation was intended to operate independently and initiate projects on its own. Just recently my husband explained once again what his reasons were for starting the Bertelsmann Foundation. No one can say it better than he can:

> Right after the war I had to take on entrepreneurial responsibilities. Therefore I never had the time nor the opportunity to go to college. As a young man I had to learn a great deal in a rather short time. I realized then that the best way to learn is to ask the advice of those who are good at what they are doing. Therefore I've always sought out the best in any given field. That's how you learn what's important without wasting your time with superficial things. And above all, when talking to an expert, you have the opportunity to correct your mistakes and grow personally. This is true for my entrepreneurial work as well as for my work in the Foundation. I devoted the decades immediately after the war to building Bertelsmann into a media enterprise. It was a difficult time, yet wonderful and full of challenges. If, as an entrepreneur, you've learned to take on complex problems,

shape a business, and find effective solutions on a daily basis, you end up looking at social and political structures in a different light. You realize that in many ways our political and social structures have not grown and changed with the times.

This discomfort with the organization of our society, which, quite frankly, every citizen of a democracy should feel, made me want to help change things for the better. My guiding principle was the responsibility every single citizen should feel towards his or her community. This is what led me to establish the Bertelsmann Foundation twenty-three years ago.

Our era is defined by the radical changes of the conditions of our lives, brought forth and shaped by an explosion of knowledge and technical possibilities. With these rapid changes we have developed new demands, new goals and new ways of life. Our cultures are no longer defined by static and stable conditions of life untouched by external conditions. Our mobility changes our world and turns it more and more into a common habitat—room for all of us to live. Cooperation as well as global competition characterize our era. Obviously this does not come to pass without dramatic tensions. We need to find new answers to the questions posed by the new conditions in our new era. And the Bertelsmann Foundation intends to help with that.

For more than twenty years the Foundation has worked as a "laboratory of reform" to help speed up the process of social innovation. The responsibilities and purposes of the Foundation include:

Supporting the media sciences, especially by making competence and responsibility the media's first and foremost goals

Researching and developing innovative concepts of leadership and organization in all areas of the economy and government

Lending advice and setting up international projects to support international cooperation in areas such as politics, education, and culture

Supporting education in general as well as developing educational systems in all subject areas; supporting measures taken for the common good in the business world

Supporting effective structures currently within our society, in international relations, the media, medicine, the economy, and business, especially by supporting research projects and the development of their concepts and goals

Supporting general measures in education, religion, culture, and international dialogue as well as in the fields of social services and health services.

In the beginning the Foundation did pioneering work. Everybody helped everybody. When, for example, materials had to be unpacked, everyone lent a hand, the boss as well as the janitor. We were a community. It was a wonderful time. Now the Bertelsmann Foundation includes approximately 230 employees working on about 180 projects in all the fields mentioned above. Our annual budget for the year 2000–2001 was about 124 million German marks (US $62 million).

My work with the Foundation allowed me to realize some of my ideas. I felt I was on the right track. I took charge of the department of medicine and health services, as well as the department of culture. From the beginning it has been my goal to create a dialogue among experts in these fields, to assimilate their knowledge and then pass it on to other specialists as well as to the media.

Today I am responsible for about fifty employees. In my personal offices alone I employ six assistants and one rather busy personal assistant. That was not my intention, but it simply turned out that way, just like many other things in my life. Step by step I followed my instincts, and I developed along the way. I was very creative, I wanted to shape things, and start new projects. I have worked hard to make things happen, and I've accepted responsibility.

The Meaning of My Life: Helping Others

A study conducted in the US has shown that helping others makes you happy. Ninety-five percent of people who have helped others feel especially good about themselves. Research has shown that this is due to endorphins released by the body when you help others. This corresponds to my experience exactly.

Shouldn't this realization make people want to help others? It would help elderly people especially, who might be able to overcome loneliness and depression. Experts believe that loneliness is the main reason for suicide. Apathy is also a very sad aspect of our society. Many people are tired of life because they have no more interests. Very little moves them, and they don't care about what happens in the world around them. Personal issues become more important than anything else, and any concerns above and beyond their own are forgotten. I believe it is this self-centered attitude that makes so many people tired, weary, and bored. Dissatisfaction and psychological problems often follow naturally.

These days it is only in a crisis that brotherly love shows its face. It is not that people have forgotten how to care about others, but rather that many people have just become too lazy. They feel that institutions like the government and the church should do the job. Such an attitude is regrettable. People who think in this way suffer from a lack of purpose, which would otherwise give them renewed strength and energy. People grow with their responsibilities. You have no time to think about yourself, no time to be in a bad mood. Your life becomes meaningful.

Loneliness and egotism isolate people and make them unhappy. How can we show people how to make their lives meaningful? My answer is clear and simple: care for others. Helping others creates a sense of mutual understanding, of unity and togetherness. Forlorn feelings and loneliness disappear, and life suddenly has a clear meaning.

For many years, both in my personal life and with my work at the Bertelsmann Foundation, I've tried to show others how to care for those in need. I've motivated all of my friends, even those who have very little time to give.

There is Roswitha Brandt, for example, an old friend of mine from my childhood. Her husband was a dentist, and she worked in his practice for many years. When he retired, she volunteered to lead three self-help groups for stroke victims in Bielefeld. She wanted to have responsibilities that were meaningful. Now she organizes vacation trips for stroke victims, visiting castles in the Münster area, and even goes bowling with them. The joy and gratefulness of the patients she works with is all the compensation she needs.

And there's my friend Anita Schmied, whom we all lovingly call "Jimmy." Every week she visits a nursing home to help care for the elderly. She talks with them, reads to them, and sings songs with them. Once I came along and we sang together. I was very touched when I noticed how much attention these people need, and how happy this attention makes them. Jimmy is always so moved when her old friends say things like, "We'll tell the big man upstairs that you are a good person." I agree with her when she says, "You yourself take something with you from the encounters with these people."

In Germany, every year about 2.6 billion hours of volunteer work are done by 22 million men and women fourteen years and older. They work in sports clubs and cultural centers, in emergency services, in youth and educational services, in churches, schools, and in social institutions. It is a number to be proud of, but there is always a need for more. Even if you have only a little time to give, you should give it to those in need. Albert Schweitzer once said, "No matter how much the suffering in the world occupies my mind, I never waste time just thinking about it. I follow the belief that every single one of us has the power to make some of this suffering disappear." This belief is the fulcrum of my work, and I see Albert Schweitzer's life as an example of practical brotherly love.

In *The Art of Loving*, Erich Fromm writes,

> The most fundamental kind of love, which underlies all types of love, is brotherly love. By this I mean the sense of responsibility, care, respect, knowledge of any other human being, the wish to further his life. . . . Brotherly love is love for all human beings; it is characterized by its very lack of exclusiveness. . . . In brotherly love there is an experience of union with all men, of human solidarity, of human atonement. Brotherly love is based on the experience that we are all one. The differences in talents, intelligence, and knowledge are negligible in comparison with the identity of the human core common to all men. In order to experience this identity, it is necessary to penetrate from the periphery to the core. If I perceive in another person mainly the surface, I perceive mainly the differences, that which separates us. If I penetrate to the core, I perceive our identity, the fact of our brotherhood.

Compassion as True Humanity

"Ask not what your country can do for you; ask what you can do for your country." John F. Kennedy's appeal during his oath for office in 1960 roused his fellow citizens. It is my belief as well. Faced with shrinking government coffers, it is more vital than ever that more people show commitment to their community.

I'm encouraged when I see how young men during their civil service[1] enthusiastically care for people who are old and sick. I remember one very spoiled young man from a rather wealthy background. I remember how his eyes would light up when talking

---

[1] In Germany young men have to do mandatory military or civil service for about 18 months.

about the old people he delivered food to for a meal service. Even on Christmas Eve he would deliver food without any complaints. He said that the months he spent doing his civil service were not wasted at all; he didn't mind missing two semesters of college. On the contrary, he felt that he learned a lot from these old people, from their experiences and wisdom. And he felt that he was amply compensated by their gratitude.

This makes me wonder whether we challenge our young people enough. Many more young people would most likely be willing to do some sort of service for the common good, women as well as the young men fulfilling their mandatory civil service. Perhaps the adults in their lives need to demand more of them and set a good example. Focusing only on an intellectual education may not allow our youth to develop their emotional intelligence. "A noble heart" is what we used to call the sum of our emotional capabilities. It is a term that seems to have disappeared from our vocabulary. It encompasses all the feelings we need to make relating to others easier and more pleasant. It includes consideration, respect, tactfulness, and love. Aren't these precisely the characteristics that seem to be missing from our young people today? Sensitivity, camaraderie, a sense of community . . . can we no longer pass on such values? We mustn't ever stop trying. It is worth it.

Seen through the eyes of love, your opponent will become your partner. That is my recipe. Whenever I meet people I try to put myself in their shoes. How does he live? What's her situation at the moment? What kinds of problems does he have? What does she wish for? That's what I'm trying to find out. Then I look at her with this background in mind, and something amazing happens: I find myself becoming more understanding and more tolerant of human weakness. All great thinkers and philosophers understood the value of love and compassion. "Love . . . absolves no beloved one from loving," Dante realized, Shakespeare claims that it is love that brings joy, and Goethe maintains that "love grants in a moment's time what pure effort may never achieve."

All of us have in common the desire for someone to love us,

someone to appreciate us, to accept us just the way we are. Imagine how much more important it is for those who are sick or weak to be accepted and loved. Why do we do so little to make this possible? Love is free. Love cannot be equated with money. Yet love and friendship can be earned, if you are willing to try. Without love our society will fall apart. It is love that moves people. It is love that makes people give without ulterior motive. It is love that makes us sacrifice ourselves for larger goals.

I want to encourage each and every citizen to take a close look at his or her home town and find out where help might be needed. There are so many institutions and clubs that will be grateful for every little bit of support, even if it is only an hour or two per week. Two hours are all it takes to go for a walk with an elderly lady from a home, to feed her dog, to run errands for her, to read to her or just talk with her to ward off her loneliness. It helps. Young families may need grandmas and grandpas to take care of their small children for a while. Kindergartens may need people to tell stories or to help with an art project. Opportunities are everywhere.

A barrier to love and the spirit of volunteerism is that most people have forgotten how to talk to one another. People barely even say "hello" or "thank you." Everyone just wants to move on, pressured to get things done. Or maybe we are afraid to be vulnerable, to admit that we are not doing so well, and that we feel lonely. Everybody thinks that they have to put on the face of success and happiness at all times. This is fatal, because it is exactly how you will become more and more isolated. Everyone needs a good friend with whom he can share joy, whom he can count on to be there in hard times. Yet you have to look for and make friends and soul mates when you don't need them to make sure they are there for you when you do. It is too late to look for friends in a crisis. But unfortunately that is the only time when many people are confronted with themselves. And that's when they fall into the abyss of loneliness.

Even among neighbors there is not enough help and assistance. Many people who have lived in the same building for years don't even know the people living around them. I feel ashamed when I read reports about an old woman who falls down and remains alone and helpless for days, or a man who is not discovered in his apartment until weeks after his death, because nobody seemed to have noticed that he was gone—incidents that prove our utter lack of compassion.

It strikes me that many people are having trouble approaching others. Again and again I see how serious and closed-off people seem to be as they race through their lives. Very rarely do people take note of one another, as if they are all lost in thought. I try to counteract this with my personal strategy of smiles. If I smile at someone, they usually smile back. Is there anything more rewarding than making someone smile? "Love opens hearts"—my mantra proves itself every single day. I consciously try to smile at people—on the streets, in the office, when visiting patients. And I'm always happy when I get a smile in return. It makes my day brighter and happier. It's a simple recipe that I heartily recommend. And it may well be your first step out of isolation and into a sense of community. A smile may grow into a little chat that may then grow into the beginning of a friendship. "Let no one think they are loved by any person when they love nobody." That is how Epictetus puts it.

I enjoy approaching people, and I have made friends like that everywhere. I met my friend Anna-Maria Aden sixteen years ago in New York. She was standing apart, lonely, in the midst of one of our travel groups. I noticed her, and started a conversation. She was from Romania and spoke very little German. That's why she had very little contact with the other women. I have made it a point to take care of her since then, and I've tried to help her get accustomed to German culture and get along in Germany. We've been friends ever since and we get along splendidly. She is full of energy and very independent. Even though she has moved to a different city, we still keep in touch.

I love people, and I want to help them in any way I can. My day starts at about seven in the morning with phone calls. Friends and acquaintances call for advice when someone in their family is ill. Or they call when they are sick themselves. I try to find them the best possible care available. Sometimes I might even send materials to America to get advice from specialists. One of my girlfriends, for example, had a very serious form of cancer. Before each treatment of chemotherapy, I sent her little presents to raise her spirits. And after her chemotherapy, I invited her and her husband to spend some time with us in our house in Mallorca so she could rest. Another girlfriend had breast cancer and was hospitalized in Düsseldorf. I organized all of our friends to take turns visiting her, to make sure she wouldn't be alone for a single day. To distract her, we'd take her out to dinner, even though she had an IV catheter in her arm. We'd just cover the capsule with a silk scarf. She had so much courage, and she made it through. Today she is healthy and very energetic. I believe the love and care she received from her friends helped. And there are many other examples like that from among my friends and acquaintances. We've always tried to be there for one another.

When I go through Gütersloh, people ask me for help. I am all ears, regardless of whether it's a grandmother who needs a wheelchair or a teenager who needs a job. I support and help as much as I can. It starts with the little things. If I see old people or children who are afraid to cross the street, I offer my arm and lead them across. It doesn't matter if I'm in a hurry. There's always got to be time for that. I cannot walk away. I think this has become second nature since my Pathfinder days.

People should give themselves firsthand experience in contributing to their community. Not only will this bolster their self-confidence, but it will also give them a sense of usefulness in their society. People should offer their assistance in areas close to home such as families, neighborhoods, clubs, offices, churches or residential communities. And it is the responsibility of our political and social leaders to create conditions that ensure, enable, and nourish life in these areas. Once we show our willingness to take responsibility and initiative, once we strive to create structures that allow us to live according to social values—only then can we ensure the common good. This is the only way for us to create a citizenry in which each member feels a responsibility for the whole. Mankind as a whole has a future only if each and every person feels a responsibility for his or her country. Our society depends on the volunteer work of the individual. Volunteering is practical democracy. Brotherly love and compassion create togetherness.

Learning By Doing

My first attempts at a professional life weren't easy. Just like anyone new on the job, I made mistakes, and I got my share of bruises. But instead of discouraging me, this challenged me. I wanted to make it. I wanted to be able to work responsibly, to create my own projects, no matter what the difficulties and setbacks might be. I've always been very curious, even as a child. Often I wondered whether I'd be able to make it, and that's what motivated me. I wanted to prove to myself that I could do it.

Of course it was tough at first to give speeches in front of large audiences. I was always nervous. But no pain, no gain. My principle was "learning by doing." You're bound to get things wrong along the way. If a speech didn't work, I knew it myself. But I'd do it again anyway, and I'd do it better the second time around. Today I speak freely before audiences of thousands with minimal notes. And I'm not that nervous doing it.

We can all learn by doing, but growing isn't easy. If you never fail, perhaps because you're afraid of the unknown, you won't grow. You won't experience your own strength or your ability to go beyond your own limitations.

It is not unusual for me to give two or more speeches per week, in front of all kinds of audiences. That's part of my job. Yet I've consciously avoided taking public speaking classes. I don't want to be a professional speaker, like a politician. I want to be my natural self, even as I lecture. I want every last member of the audience to know that I am serious about the issue at hand. I want to reach the hearts of people, and I want to be credible. I believe you need to show true human emotion to achieve this, not polished and perfect rhetoric. After all, perfectionism is sterile and lacks warmth.

For some time now my daily agenda has been that of a manager. I get up at around six-thirty in the morning and exercise diligently for about an hour and a half. I'm at the office by ten every morning, and I participate in meetings and conferences relating to all aspects of our company's business. I also plan and manage my own projects, prepare for meetings with business associates, visit self-help groups, and meet with potential sponsors of my Foundation. I rarely get home before nine at night. I never expected that at first. But I grew with my work, and slowly I became more self-confident and independent.

My eyes are always open. I constantly try to collect ideas for projects our Foundation can help realize. I do so to this day. Since I am a communicative person, I hear about the anxieties and problems of our employees, as well as those of our friends and family. I meet politicians and businesspeople in the course of my work. I take ideas from everyone back to the Foundation.

I am in charge of the field of culture, and my goal is to support music and musical education, to develop opportunities to support new vocal talent in a realistic and efficient manner, and to create an open dialogue among culture, the economy, politics and media. This was true for my first project as well. In 1987 I started the international singing contest, New Voices.

4. New Voices

Those who sing or play an instrument speak a second language.

The language of music is inexhaustible in its variety, it breaks down walls of loneliness, it brings people together.

—former German president Roman Herzog

Every other year the Gütersloh town hall and the city theater become a magical place for me. I try to spend every free minute there. From far away I hear the singing and playing as it echoes through windows and doors out into the town square. I hear beautiful soprano voices accompanied by piano, then I hear a baritone or bass. I hear young people training the most precious instrument—their own voices. These sounds move me immensely. As soon as I dive into the darkness of the auditorium I'm enchanted by the music and the beautiful voices. The daily grind seems far away, I forget all problems and pressures, and I allow myself to be enveloped in the tones as they shape their melodies. It is the time of our international singing competition *Neue Stimmen,* or New Voices, which has been taking place in Gütersloh for the past fifteen years.

Former German president Roman Herzog was right in his assessment of the power of music. The list of wise thoughts about the nature and significance of music for mankind is endless. I believe that music is an intrinsic part of human nature. Music is one of our basic needs; it is food for the soul. Without music our lives would be empty and desolate. A day without music is a lost day. Studies of tribal cultures illustrate that there is a strong natural inclination to express yourself through singing and rhythm, because in those cultures music is an integral part of all rituals.

Every day you can see that music knows no borders. Music is everywhere. Never before have so many people turned to music. Similar to our efforts at fostering reading at Bertelsmann, we've also been trying to do similar things in the world of music. Therefore it seemed perfectly natural that the Foundation should sponsor a music project.

There is a story to New Voices. In 1985 we invited conductor Herbert von Karajan and the Berlin Philharmonic to give a concert at the town hall in Gütersloh in honor of the 150th birthday of the house of Bertelsmann. It was a lovely guest appearance, and it made the event quite glamorous. Later, during dinner, the maestro mentioned how difficult it was to find young opera talent. What they were missing were "new voices."

His remark pricked my ears. I just couldn't get it out of my mind. Was there a way that the Bertelsmann Foundation could help with that? Could we foster new vocal talent? I asked my husband what he thought of this idea. He thought it was terrific.

Who was the right person to talk to about this? The person who immediately came to mind of course was our lively and vital Professor August Everding, then General Director of the Bavarian theaters. He was a man of irresistibly persuasive powers, full of charm and humor. He was a tireless and eloquent promoter of the arts, earning him the journalistic title of "Mr. Theater." He knew the cultural landscape like no one else. Wearing many different hats, he was, at various times, the president of the German Stage Association, the International Institute for Theater, the Bavarian Academy for the Theater, and the Opera Convention, among others. He was the right man to turn to in order to start something new. He had the necessary courage and creativity, and he would become one of the major supporters of our new project.

I had met him at several previous events, so I called him up. "Professor Everding," I said, " I have an idea. I'd like to meet with you to discuss it over dinner. Perhaps you have an idea as well.

And if we put our ideas together, perhaps something extraordinary will come about." Professor Everding agreed to meet with me immediately. We had dinner in Munich.

It was always a pleasure to dine with August Everding. But that aside, this particular meeting had a positive outcome. He told me that worldwide there was no competition for new voice talent that was accompanied by an orchestra. The idea was to put together a competition that would simulate the very conditions a singer might meet during a "real" performance: a large stage to be filled with stage presence, an auditorium to resonate with their voices, and a full orchestra instead of just the usual piano. This was a pioneering idea. Nothing like it existed. Usually, auditions take place in cold, dusty, dark rooms. Such an atmosphere is not very inspiring to young talent.

And so, in cooperation with the German Stage Association which August Everding chaired at the time, the international singing competition New Voices came into being. He took over the presidency of the jury, and until his death in 1999 he continued to make his mark on every aspect of the event. He gave us many unforgettable and beautiful hours.

In 1993 Professor Gustav Kuhn of the Accademia di Montegral, president of the Tyrolean Festival, took over the creative leadership of our competition. My husband had known him since childhood; his father used to work in our book club in Salzburg.

Our goal was to create positive conditions for national and international careers, something like the "Olympic Games" of beautiful voices. The idea was that an audience of experts would make this event a stock market for young talent. We hoped that TV coverage and the presence of other media would support the new talent and create career opportunities. Above all, we wanted this event to improve international communication and cooperation. Female vocalists under thirty and male vocalists under thirty-two were encouraged to participate, if their talent portended an international career.

About our first competition in 1987 my husband remarked, "We strive to reach a worldwide audience. We believe that a more intensive cultural collaboration will create the conditions for understanding and harmony among all people of the world. The Bertelsmann Foundation has called for a European vocal competition in order to foster cultural contact within Europe. We want to reveal our common interests, and we hope that this meeting of artists and representatives of cultural institutions will bring forth new ideas, and will start careers."

Thirty-six participants from Europe and throughout the world—Germany, Switzerland, Bulgaria, France, Poland, Italy, Austria, Sweden, England, the United States, Canada, South Korea and Japan—participated in our first event. The applicants had to study and perform three arias from a classical repertory of opera and operetta. This was true in the beginning and is still the case today. The competition always ends with two concerts. The first concert presents the sixteen semi-finalists, and the final concert presents the eight finalists. These concerts are always very festive. About 900 guests from politics, culture, business, and the entertainment industry are usually invited. And of course the music industry is represented as well.

What good is great talent, if you don't get the chance to show it on stage? Our New Voices competition was meant to help promising voices find venues where they'd put their talent to work. The auditions, during which the voices are accompanied only by a piano, take place in a large concert hall, rather than in a small room. We hire full orchestras for the final concerts in order to create conditions that are as realistic as possible. We invite German directors, agents from all over Europe, and representatives of the music industry, as well as journalists from radio, TV, and the press. All this helps the vocalists to get a contract. The final concerts receive TV and radio coverage. They are even recorded and can be purchased on CD.

The Significance of Competitions

Do competitions make sense? The psychological stress within the brief moments of an audition is very intense. Many performers fail. Nonetheless, the answer is clear: Yes, competitions are necessary, and they do make sense. There is no other way to separate the wheat from the chaff among the new talent.

Artists, directors, agents, and managers—in short, all experts from the world of theater—are occupied more and more with the arduous search for new talent. In search of the star of tomorrow, they observe master classes, visit international competitions, and sit through final concerts. That is where the up-and-coming voices display their talents. These young vocalists face challenges and take risks, each one hoping that their final concert will make their career and start their future as a soloist. Anxiety, stage fright, and technical competence play a role—some demonstrate incredible technical virtuosity, some charm with their personality or with their creativity.

Competitions are a form of quality control. It is as important for the talent as for the casting offices. Competitions reveal the level of each participant's technique. Musical life cannot exist without a high standard of expertise. Our society depends on such expertise, and the arts are no different.

But competitions serve yet another purpose. Illusions run high in artistic circles. A competition may reveal, before it's too late, whether a young artist has the talent and stamina it takes to make it. Perhaps the young artists will realize whether they have what it takes to deal with the growing demands of the career they are about to embark on.

A beautiful performance requires that musician and music be one. The quality of the presentation is more important now than ever. The media require that a vocalist develop new skills—the skills of an entertainer and a star. No vocalist can depend on musical talent alone anymore. A good voice needs to be paired with acting skills and stage presence. The fascism of physical beauty reigns the stage as well. You cannot fake it, since we live in the spotlight of the media. Any competition must acknowledge these developments in the music industry. This is why the vocalists in our competitions encounter concert conditions that are realistic.

The demands above and beyond a good voice are great. The young vocalists must be able to communicate in several languages, they must be familiar with many different styles and genres, they must understand what it is they are singing about (that is truly important), and they must express their personality.

"Personality before perfection," Professor Everding would always say. "The individual expression is what counts. We are looking for young talent who can sing an aria beautifully, but in a way we have never heard it before. It's a new interpretation we are looking for rather than a sensational one. I am looking for that unique talent, for the vocalist I can see even when I close my eyes."

Experts say again and again that a great career has to be built slowly, and a competition is nothing but a springboard. Here's an example: In early 1961 a twenty-five-year-old tenor from Modena won the Peri Prize in the town of Piacenza. Part of the prize was the chance to debut at the Teatro Municipael de Reggio Emilia, singing the role of Rodolfo in *La Bohème*. The young tenor was so inexperienced that the director had to tell him not to hug his Mimi while singing so that they'd both still be able to breathe well enough to sing. A typical beginner's mistake. The young tenor I am talking about was Luciano Pavarotti. It was still another five years until his debut at La Scala in Milano, ten more years until his tremendous success at the Met in New York, and twenty more years until popular stardom. This is how it goes, even for a vocalist of exceptional talent. Success takes time.

Competitions are traditional and are a springboard for careers—to this very day.

A Tough Process of Selection

There is a greater need for good voices than ever before. The number of opera houses and festivals has increased, opera seasons are longer, and recording studios are always in need of more and more new voices. Many directors cast by a specific type rather than by individual voice criteria. There are egocentric conductors, who push their desires through without regard for the vocal nature of a singer, and who care very little about the fact that they may destroy voices and careers that way. The wear and tear in the audio-visual media is so great that it is almost impossible to nurture and grow a talent. There is a real danger that talented vocalists will burn out before they've had a chance to mature, since early on they are cast in roles that cannot be handled by talent alone. Some roles need the experience of many years on stage. Therefore students have to learn that it may be just as critical *not* to take an opportunity as it is to take it at the right time. For this reason, our exceptionally competent jury is willing to give advice on how to manage a career. Over the years, members of our jury have included such people as Elisabeth Schwarzkopf, Brigitte Fassbaender, Reri Grist, Erika Köth, Edda Moser, Birgit Nilsson, Hellmuth Matiasek, Francisco Araiza, Sir George Christie, Gundula Janowitz, Sir John Tooley, Hans Hirsch, Christoph Groszer and René Kollo.

Many of the young vocalists use our competition to see where they are in their careers. They want to know how far they've come, but many participate too early. They audition with an unsuitable repertory and an immature presentation. Some don't yet know how to present themselves. Often it takes a year or two to see which direction a career will take. It is the purpose of the Foundation to give these multitalented young people opportunities to go beyond the competition itself. We offer advice on many career issues. We offer the opportunity to participate in master classes, where they can work on their vocal presentation as well as on their stagecraft without the psychological strain of an actual performance. A career won't go anywhere without self-confidence, charisma, and stage presence. Our artistic director, Gustav Kuhn, has often noticed that some of the talent who don't even make the first round of our competition have nonetheless shown incredible promise. A good psychological condition is an integral part of competition. Without the stress of public performance, many a vocal talent is able to develop in a master class.

The goals of all our master classes are to support the development of promising talent, to further singers' careers, and to foster personal development. The Egyptian participants were a good example of raw talent. When they started with us, Professor Everding would say with friendly sarcasm, "There is still desert sand on their vocal cords." They had beautiful but untrained voices. One of the vocalists, for example, learned how to sing from a CD because she couldn't find a teacher. But she had so much talent that she could successfully participate in our master class.

Our main focus is: discussions with the jury and artistic directors; mentoring individual vocalists while soliciting sponsors for them; one-week master classes that include a final concert, three-day workshops with full orchestra and usually in co-operation with the WDR.[2]

Whenever my time permits, I listen to the concerts and the master classes. The conditions are tough, I admit. It's not easy singing an aria early in the morning when the voice isn't smooth yet, in an empty room and accompanied only by a grand piano rather than a whole orchestra. You can actually hear how tough it is. Many of them sing as if their life depended on it. Then out of nowhere a tenor appears, and you think you're in paradise. It is such a joy to hear these voices from all over the world.

It is not without pride that I say I've listened well. My evaluation of a voice usually coincides with that of the expert jury. Such

[2] WDR = *Westdeutscher Rundfunk*, one of the public German TV and radio stations.

was the case, for example, of the contralto Nathalie Stutzman, who has since become a renowned concert vocalist. She has recorded with the Bertelsmann Music Group more than a dozen times. She placed first in our debut competition in 1987. Yet she didn't win unanimously. "She sings like a man," some of our jurors said. But I voted for her. And, as time has shown, I was right.

Of course, something goes wrong at every competition. In October 1999, for example, the Bulgarian participants lost their suitcases. We had to get appropriate clothing for these young people, because they had arrived in chilly Gütersloh in nothing but summer clothing and sandals. It was fall, after all. In their home town Sofia, however, it had still been rather warm when they left. Some of the young women often need the assistance of my tailor to make alterations to their dresses. We don't mind organizing that at all.

Many young men from the East show up in tuxedos, many women in festive evening gowns. Young people from the West, on the other hand, often show up in jeans and a T-shirt. They don't understand the significance of a dress code. They seem to have forgotten that a lack of form can be a sinfully big mistake for an artist. In America, a certain "flair" in performance is regarded as important. An appropriate presentation is part of the skill and duty of the artist. Numerous times our employees had to find evening gowns for some of the ladies and thus were able to contribute to their success.

Italian Andrea Silvestrelli went down in our annals as the "sneaker man." During his performance, he wore sneakers with his tuxedo. We were rather surprised by his taste. But then we learned that he had left his shoes at home, and all he could find on such short notice in his size in Gütersloh were sneakers.

Once, a young Russian lost his suitcase, and with it his sheet music. We had to get him new music in a hurry. The poor man was so nervous during warm-up. "I won't make it anyway," he said as he went onto the stage. It turned out that he was right. I felt so bad for him. But the jury decided against him. Not everyone can win, even though I wish it for all of the participants. Maybe he'll have better luck in another competition.

It makes me happy to see that young vocalists are friendly with each other, and feel nervous for each other despite their competitiveness. I guess they grow into a small family over the days of the competition. They're all in the same boat. They make contacts, maybe even friends. They exchange addresses and take pictures. There is a colorful mixture of languages, yet they communicate successfully. I enjoy watching how much enthusiasm, heart, and courage these young people show when they make music.

Some of the young people meditate before their performance. One young Asian performer once told me, "The most difficult part is getting in touch with the atmosphere and emotions of the particular scene before you're actually performing. You have to isolate yourself from external circumstances. You cannot be distracted." Others pray, hug each other, or spit over each other's shoulders before they go on stage. Some hold a crumpled tissue in their hands, as if it could give them support. I feel with them every single time. I cross my fingers when I see how nervous those young men and women are at their auditions. You can actually sense the creative tension in the air.

I enjoy listening to the stories of what brought these young people to their art. One young American once told me that he had had the loudest voice in his high-school choir. His music teacher told him, "Go to the doctor or take singing lessons." Another young female vocalist openly admitted that her soul would break apart without singing. And yet others conceded that indeed it hurts a little bit when you are confronted with someone who is better than you. I can relate to all of that.

But all of them, whether they win prizes or not, will collect valuable experiences. And that may help them do better at the next competition.

The European Competition Becomes an International Talent Market

Over the years, our European competition grew into an international talent market. In these times of political and economic instability, we are facing constant changes of our political map, due to the breakdown of old political systems and the birth of new nations. New spiritual direction and identification with common goals are more important than ever. The cultural exchange has assumed an important role of integration and offers a forum for new contacts and encounters with all cultures, beyond the limitations of nationalism.

After the fall of the Iron Curtain, previously unknown resources of vocal talent from the East became available. In 1991, vocalists from the new German states and the former Soviet countries participated. For example, a whole group of singers from Odessa, Minsk, Moscow, and Leningrad auditioned, exhibiting an amazingly high skill level.

Internationalization and the growing openness of the East began to influence and shape the face of our competition. In 1993, Moscow put together its first round of preliminary auditions. And in 1995 we began to work with the Yokusada Art Theater Foundation in Japan, which made it possible for 150 applicants from Asia to meet. They were from Korea, Taiwan, Japan, and Indonesia, further proof of international collaboration nurtured by the competition. The participants who qualify for the finals perform before an audience of more than eighteen hundred visitors. At the same time we offered an open voice class under the direction of Gustav Kuhn and the idolized Japanese impresario Kiyoshi Igarashi. More than three hundred people were in the audience.

Bulgaria, Mexico, and the People's Republic of China held their first preliminary rounds in 1997. In a country like China, which is about twenty-six times the size of Germany, distances alone make any talent search difficult. The Chinese Cultural Ministry in Beijing, however, did a perfect job of supporting and organizing the preliminary rounds. We were surprised by the amount of interest, especially since Western music is not yet readily available everywhere. Some vocalists, so I heard, had studied their parts from CDs, because they couldn't find any teachers. Gustav Kuhn, who was in charge of the preliminary auditions there, said, "I asked the Chinese why they are interested in European opera. Their answer was that they need our music for educational purposes, because it forms people in a way they consider appropriate. They felt that rock and pop, however, have an adverse effect on young people's development." More than one hundred male and female vocalists auditioned in the People's Republic of China. Eighteen made it to the final round in Beijing. The jury consisted of the presidents of the two great academies of music in Shanghai and Beijing, as well as two of their renowned professors of music and voice. Professor Kuhn represented the Bertelsmann Foundation.

During the preliminary rounds in Beijing, the brilliant voice of one twenty-three year old bass caught everyone's attention. His name was Li Xiaoliang. Although he was working full-time as a teacher, he took singing lessons, sacrificing greatly to finance them. Speaking not a word of English or German, he made his way from Beijing to Gütersloh for the final rounds. It was the first time he had traveled outside of China, so this was his very first contact with Western culture. His exceptional talent earned him not only a prize, but also a place in the master class.

Participation in our competition is greatly sought after, as is illustrated by the preliminary rounds in Bulgaria, which were supported by the Music Academy of Sofia. The jury was expecting nineteen vocalists, and ninety showed up. They had heard about our event through the grapevine. The jury had to go through a marathon of auditions late into the night, but they listened to every one of the ninety applicants.

Successful Participants

We are rather proud of the careers on which our participants and prize recipients have embarked. One of the most prominent winners of our competition is Vesselina Kasarova from Bulgaria. Her participation in New Voices in 1989 launched an international career: She signed with the Bertelsmann Music Group in New York, and accepted an engagement with the Zürich Opera. She has become an opera star who is very much in demand on many of the world's stages. Bass René Pape from Dresden, who won first place in 1989, has embarked on an international career as well. He's had engagements at La Scala, in Salzburg, and in Bayreuth.

Russian Eteri Gvasava from Omsk was the winner of our 1997 competition, as well as being named Voice of the Year. She was twenty-seven at the time. She won the jury over with the Mimi aria from Puccini's *La Bohème*, and took home 15,000 German marks (US $7,000) and our trophy—a golden tuning fork. Later, speaking rather frankly in an interview, she said that often a job in Western Europe is the only hope for a Russian artist. She feels fortunate to have been able to sing the role of Fiordiligi in Mozart's *Così fan tutte* produced by Giorgio Strehler at the Teatro Piccolo in Milan, Italy. It was the last directorial work of this great man of theater. It was taped for TV and recorded for radio, and had been shown and played forty-three times between January and March. A re-recording has been planned. Eteri Gvasava has also sung Fiordiligi at the Teatro Communale in Bologna, Italy, under the direction of Daniele Gatti, Italy's new premier conductor. She was able to go straight from these Italian guest appearances to her first steady engagement as a lyric soprano at the opera in Bielefeld. This contract was offered to her immediately after the competition. This example shows how much small opera houses depend on our competition in their search for new talent. After only two seasons, Eteri Gvasava had outgrown the small roles. She moved on to singing the role of

Tatiana in Tchaikovsky's *Eugene Onegin*, and the role of the slave Liu in Puccini's *Turandot*. In the TV movie, *La Traviata à Paris*, she sang the lead. What a wonderful success story!

When meeting Eteri Gvasava later, she approached me after a performance with a huge smile and thanked me and my husband for giving her the opportunities she'd had. Such moments are the highlights of my professional life. Is anything more worthwhile than helping develop a young person's talents?

Gvasava openly discussed what she felt during the competition. "Every competition is like a game of roulette," she said. "You hope and you are nervous, but you never know what may happen. But I was calm, because I'd had my final examination at the music school on the very day I left for Gütersloh, so I got rid of all my jitters right there. I have to be honest," she continued, "New Voices was the most strenuous competition I'd ever participated in at the time. It was a very tough test. On the one hand, it is very difficult; yet, on the other hand, you mobilize your entire physical potential. It's good to know what you can do, and what you cannot do."

And there are many other success stories. Endrik Wootrich made it to the final rounds, yet he didn't win a prize. Today, however, he is one of the best German tenors. Marina Ivanova, our first place winner of 1993, received an engagement at the opera in Essen. The English tenor Gwen-Hughes Jones, prize winner in 1995, belonged to the ensemble of the Welsh National Opera for a while, and he also appeared in Salzburg. Roman Trekel, finalist in 1989 (he didn't win a prize) has become an ensemble member at the State Opera in Berlin. And let's not forget baritone Falk Struckmann, who sang *Wozzeck* in Berlin as well as at the Met, and who recorded *Wozzeck* under the direction of Daniel Barenboim.

Every year there are young participants at the competition whom I will never forget, because they have grown so dear to me. One of them is seventeen-year-old Korean Yu-Ye-Kim, who in 1997 participated in the Japanese preliminary rounds when she was barely fourteen years old. I noticed her, the promising young child with the beautiful voice. Last year she participated in our master class in Japan. She was just darling in her white dress and red roses, holding a lit candle in her hand. She reminded me of a little elf. This year I invited her to sing at the opening concert in the hall of Alcudia on Mallorca, organized by Bertelsmann. It was a nice accomplishment for her, and she wrote a touching letter of thanks to me. I will keep watching her and try to sponsor her.

I've followed the development of Russian Tatjana Woropai with great interest. Her trip from Siberia to Gütersloh took more than two days by rail. Barely a one of our young people in Western Europe would go through such a long and strenuous trip just to get to a competition. She arrived in torn jeans and unkempt hair, her face hidden behind huge glasses. It hurt to see her that way. In such a state, this talented and pretty girl would not have had a chance in the competition. So, I arranged for a stage dress from the Bielefeld Theater to be delivered to her, sent her to the hairdresser, and hired a makeup artist for her. Just before she went on stage, I took her glasses away. The ugly duckling had turned into a swan. She still keeps in touch with me, writing about the engagements she has had since then.

Our eighth competition, in 1999, saw 1,022 participants from forty-six nations audition. Sixty candidates made it to the final rounds. Preliminary rounds were held worldwide—in Berlin, Buenos Aires, London, Madrid, Milan, Moscow, Munich, New York, Paris, Beijing, Pretoria, Sofia, Stockholm, Tokyo, and Warsaw. This is how international our competition has become.

Gustav Kuhn and Brian Dickie, general manager of the Chicago Opera Theater, were in charge of the preliminary rounds. Brian Dickie alone listened to more than 900 voices. For each competition the preparations take about a year and a half. In summer we send out thousands of invitations for the actual event in fall. An invitation to one of the two final concerts is very sought after. In addition to the media, the directors and the music experts, we also invite representatives of local businesses in Gütersloh and Bielefeld. They are dedicated sponsors, and they support me in any way they can. I want to thank them from the bottom of my heart.

A Glittering Party

The 1999 participants had to deal with our new artistic concept, to create conditions that are even closer to those of a real stage performance. Under the direction of Gustav Kuhn, the sixteen finalists who had made it through the preliminary rounds took a master class to work on their artistic presentation. An exceptional jury chose three winners from among these male and female opera singers. Gustav Kuhn introduced a new point system that, not unlike that of a skating competition, distinguished mandatory technical skills from "free," or interpretative, skills. A singer's technique is a mandatory skill, while his or her stage presence is considered a free skill. This made the competition more lively, colorful, and interesting.

Nineteen young artists from eleven countries performed in the final concert. In 1999, twenty-eight-year-old Tina Schlenker was the first German participant to ever win the New Voices competition. She won over both audience and jury alike with her performances of the roles of Zerlina from Mozart's *Don Giovanni* and Zerbinetta from *Ariadne auf Naxos*. Kuhn called this a "dream decision." Tina Schlenker is a lyrical coloratura soprano, and she studied at the music academy in Freiburg. She is presently under contract with the State Theater in Braunschweig. René Kollo, who became president of the jury after August Everding's death, said, "I am proud that a vocalist from our country has won the competition. She really did a good job."

The glittering party after the final concert at the Parkhotel in Gütersloh is always the high point of the competition. Artists and guests are invited together. The atmosphere is so happy and casual, you can tell that the young people have finally shed the stress and tension of the competition. They mix and mingle in small groups, sipping champagne and getting along in spite of their different nationalities. Of course, here and there you can see the face of disappointed hopes. But late at night, at the grand piano, the unofficial finale takes place. The young people sing one aria after another. Their joy is contagious. Guests stop talking and swing along to the rhythm of familiar melodies. Some even sing along. Shining eyes, beaming faces, and hugs unite quarreling politicians, directors, artists, and invited guests. They all sing together, and you can tell how much they enjoy it.

When I get home in the early morning hours, I'm usually exhausted, yet also proud and happy that I have brought joy to people, and that I've brought friends and acquaintances together from many different countries.

The very next day the work goes on. In a conference with jury members and employees, we discuss what improvements we can make at the next New Voices competition. Constructive criticism is a good way to ensure constant improvement.

Art and culture are valuable on their own. That was August Everding's credo. "That is why public sponsorship is so important." He felt that the Bertelsmann Foundation did an exceptional job and was a role model. "The secret recipe for success of the Foundation is to demand a lot from those it sponsors. Such a competition helps young artists to find the courage it takes to go the extra mile. Today's society needs this more than ever."

The magic of music crosses all borders, builds bridges, and touches the heart. Music creates a sense of community, and therefore is meaningful to any society and to mankind as a whole. The participation of fifty nations underlines the unifying character of the competition. Music and culture bring people together, build bridges of understanding, and nurture tolerance. If we get to know each other better, we will start to tolerate each other. We will no longer be fearful of new mentalities, foreign languages, different religions, and unknown cultures. Music is the language of the world—it brings together all who participate.

Musical Education in Kindergarten and Elementary School

In 1998 I initiated another project of the Bertelsmann Foundation to foster musical education in kindergarten and elementary schools. This has a story as well, a story that illustrates how I work.

We were singing Christmas carols during a Christmas party with employees of the Bertelsmann administration and the Bertelsmann Foundation. While I was singing with all my heart, I noticed that many of the young people in our group remained silent. I wondered whether they were embarrassed to sing along. When I asked, many of them had to admit that they didn't know the songs. They apparently never learned them, neither at school nor at home. They told me that they never sang together at home, not even as children.

I found their answer shocking. I consider singing to be one of the most basic communal experiences for children. We will lose a part of our culture if we stop teaching our children how to make music and how to sing. "Singing is the first language of man," says Hermann Rauhe, president of the Academy for Music in Hamburg. "Speaking comes much later, because it depends on conceptual thinking. Music creates a sense of community which cannot be compared to anything." This describes exactly what I felt as a child when we were singing in our Pathfinder group.

I will never forget what a twelve-year-old girl once told me. After school she plays in an amateur recorder group. She says that on those days she is usually in especially good spirits, because after playing the recorder for an hour or so she feels so good. The little girl obviously senses the positive influence of making music with others. It liberates the soul.

Why do our children lose interest in singing and making music? When I tried to find an answer to this question, I found that in our schools 80 percent of music classes are either cancelled or are taught by teachers without any background in the subject. I thought back to the many times that I would sing to the sound of a guitar with my Pathfinder friends or at home with my mother. These are memories I wouldn't want to miss for anything, and we should not withhold similar experiences from our children.

Music is food for the soul. It is part of our lives, and an integral aspect of human nature. Music heals: It can bring people back from a coma, it can nurture psychological stability, and it can counteract aggression. Just think about how much music helps you to relax after a tough day and how it helps you to deal with your feelings. This is reason enough for me to work hard for the support of our musical culture.

Hearing is our first sense, already fully developed in the fifth month of fetal development. Thus we can hear voices and tones rather early. Nurturing of musical talent should begin during toddlerhood. This will stimulate and strengthen a child's zest for life, and develop the child's emotional strength. Musical education should be a primary part of our kindergartens and elementary schools.

Musical education supports fantasy, creativity, and productivity. Music influences the joy of movement, singing, and creative expression. Music increases our sense of community, and thus has a positive effect on social behavior. Music loosens and liberates— I was able to notice this during New Voices quite well. Making music can foster mutual understanding, for through music we can communicate with one another emotionally, without the need for words. Musical education is very important in nurturing the development of a child's personality. In our high-tech world it is especially vital that our children have the opportunity to learn with all of their senses. Musical training develops the creative skills of our children, increases their ability to survive, inspires varied forms of creative expression, arouses the joy of music, and inspires movement to music. A musical education will encourage, maintain, and increase the joy of singing, of making and listening to music. This takes quite a bit of musical skill and knowledge on the part of the teachers. We want to help train them.

These were the thoughts that started an educational initiative in cooperation with the state government of the German state of North-Rhine Westphalia. We set up a unique model that will bring new ideas to musical education, and the Bertelsmann Foundation offered 2.5 million German marks (US $1.25 million) for this initiative. The goal is to develop new pedagogical concepts for musical education, concepts that will communicate the joy of music to children and parents alike. The project will span five years in five elementary schools in North-Rhine Westphalia. These schools will work closely with nearby kindergartens in order to develop the didactics and methods for the musical education of the little ones. Pedagogues and educators will learn to bring children to music in an age-appropriate and playful manner. One focus of this project is the incorporation of different kinds of musical styles. Pop, musicals, and folk music are simply part of our children's lives, and it is only when we take their music seriously that we can motivate them in their musical pursuits.

At the center of this project is the training of teachers and educators. Seminars not only provide information, but also practical training in such areas as vocalization and instrumentation, in music appreciation, music theory, and even in music and movement. We also offer training in accompaniment, improvisation, rhythm, musical imagery, performance art, and playful approaches to music. And, of course, singing and instrumental classes are offered for children and their parents. All educators and teachers participating in this program have the opportunity to take voice classes and guitar lessons. Teachers and educators are also encouraged to approach and maintain contact with their local musical academies.

I had help from so many experts when putting together this project: the German pop musician Peter Maffay, whom I know very well and who loves music very much; the state secretary

Wolfgang Meyer-Hesemann from the educational ministry in North-Rhine Westphalia; the renowned music critic Jürgen Kesting; the TV anchor Uwe Hübner; Viva head[3] Dieter Gorny; and Thomas M. Stein from the Bertelsmann Music Group. As Peter Maffay says, "I'd rather people sing badly than not at all."

[3] Viva Media AG is a German media corporation.

5. A Woman's Role and the
Value of Family

I was so happy to see that New Voices caught on so well. My first project was a great success for the young vocalists, for the Bertelsmann Foundation, and for me personally as well. And I have to say I am proud of that. As a result, I became more and more independent. Of course, this changed my relationship with my husband. We both had to get used to the fact that I now had my own responsibilities and my own opinions, and would even say "no" once in a while. It was a process of adaptation. We had to face each other and learn to accept each other all over again. The sweet little girl had grown into an independent woman, and we had become equal partners.

There are some men who will not accept independence and self-confidence in their wives. They fight with them and humiliate them for fear of losing the superiority that comes with the traditional role of the breadwinner. Many men constrict their wives, for they feel that the woman should serve the man. To this day you can see examples of how tragic this can be for a relationship. Studies show that if a husband refuses to share his power, it is four times more likely that the marriage will fail.

My husband didn't react this way. He's been thrilled by my development from the very beginning. He is grateful for our partnership and the way it has been growing. He has always said that it is the most precious gift of his life. We both feel that way, and we are grateful for that.

The simple truth is that a happy marriage must be based on a deep sense of friendship. Not only do husband and wife need to respect each other and hold each other in high regard, they also need to thoroughly enjoy each other's company. Both partners need to try to understand and accept each other's personality. Nobody is perfect, and everybody has shortcomings. If we always remember that, we will be able to develop intimacy and trust. It is important to show you care often, not with big presents on big occasions, but with the small things. What I mean to say is that it is important to be there for each other, to talk and to listen, to give each other tokens of appreciation, and to share intimate gestures of tenderness. My husband listens to me when I tell him about my dreams, and he listens when I'm sad. My husband is a very sensitive man. He is sensitive enough to find the right word in any situation.

I believe that a woman's independence from her husband builds a solid basis for a successful marriage. A woman needs to be independent—even if it's only earning pocket money to spend as she wishes. I recommend it highly to every woman as a means of feeling more self-confident. It's not good if, in a relationship, one partner is dependent on the other. Many people use the other's dependence to fuel their own lust for power, and the relationship suffers. It is much better if both partners have their space.

A good relationship needs constant dialogue. By that I mean intimate and open conversations. If you are able to talk with each other, not only about day-to-day issues, but also about your feelings and your hopes, you will build a solid basis for a lifelong partnership. Respect and love will grow.

Your choice of partner will influence your life. The right spouse will support, foster, and stimulate your good qualities, whereas the wrong spouse will stifle your development. I've always told my children that they should look for character when they're choosing their spouse. Every spouse needs to be able to live life independently. I wasn't at all surprised that my two sons wanted to marry professional women. Obviously they've been influenced by their parents' example. We also made sure, when raising our children, that even the boys had "kitchen duty." In Mallorca, when our staff has a day off, our boys do their share of housework as a matter of course—they clear the table, put the dishes in the dishwasher, and do laundry. They even had to learn cooking in college. Quite frankly, I think they are better cooks than I am.

Supporting Professional Women

These days women have so many more opportunities—and challenges. I experienced this firsthand. After all, not only was I the mother of three, but also a wife, a manager, and a professional host at the same time. Stress times three. Sometimes it was tough to do justice to all three responsibilities. I have to admit that I understand men much better now. It is not easy for a man, after spending a day's worth of energy and patience on professional challenges in the office, to come home and suddenly become the loving husband and father.

Since I've been working, I haven't always been able to make the switch that easily, either. At first my children shed a lot of tears, because I spent more time at the office and, therefore, less time at home. Of course, I was lucky that my office was so close to my home, so I could run home if there was any trouble. At the very beginning of my professional life, while vacationing in Switzerland, my husband took the children aside and explained why I was working. He told them that it was important to me personally, and it was important to the company as well, because he needed me there. He was very convincing. After this talk, the fact that I was working was no longer an issue for the children.

Being a woman has never been as easy as it is today, but at the same time it has never been as difficult. This generation of women has more opportunities than ever, and more household gadgets than ever to relieve the workload. When I think of how hard housework was for my mother's generation. . . . Compared to that, women today live in paradise, what with all the gadgets available. But we have to deal with different challenges. We are faced with the agony of choice. Many women today want everything: a career, a husband, and children. This takes a lot of organization, energy, and strength.

Being a professional can fulfill many needs in a woman's life. A woman can develop her interests and abilities, make friends, and build a social network. A woman's work can provide meaning for her entire life. The more content a woman is, the more the entire family will benefit, because she will be a happier wife and mother.

Of course, on the other hand, there are many women who have no choice but to work simply in order to make ends meet, to say nothing of fulfilling their family's needs and wishes.

Many women still complain about a lack of equality in the professional world, and clearly they should. In Germany, the income of female employees equals only about 83 percent of the income of male employees. According to statements released by Germany's Federal Office of Statistics, the average gross income of the male workforce was about 5,559 German marks (US $3,000), whereas women only made about 4,316 German marks (US $2,500) on average. Female employees in leadership positions are disadvantaged as well, even though they are compensated according to rates other than those agreed upon by unions. Female managers in Germany make about 20 percent less per month than their male counterparts.

According to personnel experts, women are too modest. They don't believe in themselves for many reasons. Men seem more self-confident and exhibit more refined and practiced presentation, communication, and negotiation skills. What adds to this situation is the fact that many women embark on a career in order to realize their own potential rather than in order to support a husband and a family. If we want to change this in future generations, women have to learn to keep up with men in professional matters.

Only 8 percent of women in the old German states and 16 percent of women in the new German states are in leadership positions. It will take quite some time before more women will reach the top, as all cultural changes take time, but I am sure we will be successful. Our country and the world as a whole will only be able to meet future challenges if we are able to tap into the full intellectual and creative potential of women.

I'm sure that entrepreneurs will realize that specifically female characteristics are very valuable. Women train with these characteristics every single day: Family life constantly requires intuition and diplomacy, a high social intelligence, and great flexibility. It is my experience that women build bridges and manage to find a common path, even when the positions seem entrenched. Some women have made it to the top of political committees to shape and participate in political power just based on quotas. I don't like that, because I believe we can make it there based on our abilities, knowledge, and productivity. Those who are good will be successful. In the end what counts is not a person's gender, but a person's ability.

I don't like the fact that some women imitate the behavior and language of their male colleagues, either. We shouldn't check our womanhood at the door to the office. I prefer a woman to be objective, competent, and charming at the same time. In that regard, Elisabeth Noelle-Neumann has always been a great role model for me. She's always been very knowledgeable with regard to the facts, yet never shrill or unfeminine. Even in her old age she likes to apply her lipstick whenever there is a pause in the conversation. This sends a clear signal: I will always remain a woman, even though I can hold my own in discussions with men.

The same is true for me. I wouldn't even dream of dressing in the usual black, gray, or navy blue, even though I often am the only woman in a committee full of men. I love my feminine suits in strong colors, and I will wear them. They signal the joy of life and mirror its variety.

Unfortunately, many women still have to learn professional conduct. Many women react in an overly sensitive manner, taking criticism personally. I have noticed that men manage to get along pretty well despite differences in opinion, and women should take their lessons from that.

I don't support the war of the sexes, and I am not one of the pugnacious warriors for women's rights. Yet I have always tried to support the rights of women and show my commitment to women's self-realization in my own small way. For example, at the time when I went back to work for Bertelsmann, it wasn't acceptable to invite women to the Bertelsmann Forum, a lecture series on current economic and social issues that was organized by our managers. But on my insistence, women were invited to attend and participate. At the time some male participants actually thought that this would devalue the events. This is how men were thinking only twenty years ago!

Looking back on the development of the last fifty years I think we have come quite a long way. Women were not allowed access to universities in Germany until one hundred years ago, and it wasn't until 1919 that German women were granted the right to vote. But today, almost half of our *Abitur*[1] holders are female, and on average they graduate with better grades than their male counterparts. About 45 percent of our college students are female, and there are women working in all professional fields, including politics, economics, science, the arts, administration, and the military. Forty percent of all physicians are female. About fifteen hundred women applied just two months after the German military accepted female applicants. Women will even be trained to be fighter pilots. Today not a single professional field is closed off to women because of their gender. Women participate successfully in polar expeditions under strenuous physical conditions, they fly into space, and they are boxers, soccer players, and pilots. The majority of women freely decide whether they want to work or stay at home. On average, women don't marry before they are twenty-eight years old, and they are able to decide if and when they will have children. On average, women are twenty-nine years old when their first child is born. In short, women are more liberated today than they've ever been before. Never before have they had the opportunity to follow their

[1] The *Abitur* is the degree earned at high school graduation.

dreams, and to develop and use their talents. This is a very positive development, and we should remember that.

"Do you like women?" I asked Henri Nannen, legendary publisher of the German weekly magazine *Der Stern*, after Bertelsmann acquired Gruner + Jahr, a publishing house in Hamburg. "Of course I like women," he answered with a smile. So I asked, "Do you employ female editors in leadership positions?" To his own surprise, Nannen had to answer in the negative. "But I like working with women." It's been many years since this conversation took place in our house on Mallorca, and since then the situation has changed. Of the twenty-five editorial leadership positions at Gruner + Jahr, nine are filled with women: *Brigitte, Brigitte Young Miss*[2], *Geo Saison, Schöner Essen*[3], *Schöner Wohnen*[4], *Decoration, Marie Claire*, and two business-to-business magazines. At Gruner + Jahr International in the US, all editors-in-chief are women. All American publishing houses that belong to the Bertelsmann empire employ many female managers.

Sixty-four percent of women in Germany work today. We've achieved quite a lot in a short period of history. I am sure that in the new millennium women will play a major role in public life. Many trend researchers even predict that male roles will change, because in order to meet the challenges of the future, we need intuition, emotional intelligence, social intelligence, and diplomacy. Those are typically female characteristics.

The Value of Family

It goes without saying that women's liberation has created problems as well. First and foremost, we now have to decide on our own how we want to live our lives. A large number of women want it all: a happy relationship, children, and a fulfilling career.

[2] *Brigitte* and *Brigitte Young Miss* are German women's magazines.
[3] A German magazine on dining.
[4] A German lifestyle magazine.

And this is where the problems start. Women today find themselves in a situation more difficult than ever before. They carry a triple load, and that can deplete all their strength and energy. Often this is the most difficult phase of a woman's life. I hear from my female colleagues how often they work until late at night to make sure things run smoothly at home: They do their ironing, they clean up, and they prepare for their children's birthday parties. Women still do the lion's share of household work. It seems that the idea of sharing duties has not quite sunk in yet, and that too many relationships don't provide the relief young professional women need. Only hesitantly do men open themselves to housework. So far—at least that's what I hear—men are not yet able to take over where women leave off when they take on the double load of work and family. Simply put, life at home still centers around the woman, and many people claim that family life suffers if a woman goes to work full-time. That will be true until men help more and take on more responsibility. In time they will get comfortable in their new role, and I hope the next generation will be successful.

Another negative development I see in our society is the diminishing sense of responsibility towards one's family. Many young men and women start a family only to leave it at the first sign of trouble. It seems that "'til death do us part" is a promise young couples no longer care to keep. The newfound independence has made it possible for women to break out of their marriages. While that can be a positive development, many young people set their expectations too high when they start a relationship. They don't see that a good relationship needs work, for no relationship works on its own, as if by magic. Three-quarters of young people want to get married and have children, but it seems to me that they want all of this without too much responsibility. So we end up with high divorce rates and changing spouses. The newest statistics reveal that nowadays one in three marriages—in cities one in two—ends in divorce. This becomes even more worrisome considering the number of minor children affected by this.

I think this is a dangerous development, not only for the couples and the children involved, but for society as a whole. Children need a secure future within a responsible relationship. Only a home full of love, comfort, and affection, a home where children receive direction from their role models, will provide children with the values they need to make judgments and decisions on their own, and the values they need to take responsibility for themselves and others. Children need this kind of spiritual direction, and both parents, mother and father, can (and must) give it.

On the other hand, of course, we cannot deny the fact that it is vital to leave a relationship if it really doesn't work anymore. But the disinterest in forging relationships among young people is rather striking. I think that the fear of commitment or past experiences of disappointment may explain this. Young people are no longer willing to suffer. They are too egotistical; they want a perfect relationship that won't require compromises. If a relationship won't meet their demands, young people would rather withdraw than get hurt and grow from the experience. Did we give our young people too much freedom? Are they no longer willing and able to make the compromises necessary for a close, lifelong relationship?

We have to make sure not to devalue the notion of family. Will we be able to maintain the tradition of family? What will a family look like in fifty years? These are worrisome questions, questions our society cannot answer at the moment.

The family unit is the foundation of our community. It is the most successful form of lifelong solidarity between young and old, strong and weak. It is the most important place to learn and practice values and beliefs. It offers protection and comfort, and teaches and gives love. Growing up in a family, every individual can discover and develop his or her talents. It is a good sign that marriage and children are still considered goals to strive for by a large group of people. The emotional safety provided by the family replenishes the strength and energy we need to cope with the growing demands of our environment and our professional world.

The family provides us with strength and support. Humans need such support, because we were not born to be alone, and our growing individualization makes emotional relations more and more important.

The family is a well of strength. I have always seen it that way for myself and my loved ones. I've always tried to promote our family's solidarity. As a large group, we get together regularly for family celebrations such as Christmas. Yet even if there's nothing to celebrate, we try to get together, or at least we try to talk with each other on the phone. Whether it's Easter, Passover, or Christmas, such family traditions are celebrations of togetherness and love. They are rituals which have been kept up over generations, and we should continue to maintain them.

The family contributes to the survival of any society's culture by passing on values and experiences from generation to generation. As a stable set of relationships, the family meets the individual's need for acceptance, and provides meaning to the individual's life. Within the family, the individual feels protected, and thus feels safe enough to express intimate feelings, both positive and negative. We regenerate and relax. In that way the family becomes tremendously valuable for any society, for the individual's regeneration and relaxation benefits the renewal of the workforce. Just imagine how many psychologists the government would have to hire in order to heal men and women and children if the institution of family were to disappear. The family is of irreplaceable value and unequaled importance. Who else could lend us a helping hand? The government can't and won't.

Family life provides all necessary social values. It provides care for the elderly and the weak, and it bears the responsibility to honor the estate and the memory of ancestors. Family life constantly demands and practices sensitivity, flexibility, creativity, communication skills, cooperation, and conflict resolution. Children develop a willingness to share and to help, and learn loyalty, justice, tolerance, modesty, and patience. Thus family life lays the foundation upon which we build our future lives as individuals. One of the first and most important emotions a child experiences is the loyalty toward and trust in his or her parents. A child's soul may be marked forever if this loyalty and trust should ever be disturbed or disappointed. This is a tremendous responsibility.

The example a father and a mother set greatly influences their children's behavior, even as teenagers or young adults. When parents act responsibly, they lay the foundation for their children's lifelong sense of responsibility.

The emotional conditions within a family will decide whether children are willing to learn from their parents' behaviors and attitudes. Just by sharing their lives with each other, parents pass on their values and norms to their children. Loyalty and mutual respect grow and develop, and the family provides a haven where deep desires as well as emotional and existential needs are fulfilled. In your family you can show yourself without a public mask, and you can experience comfort like nowhere else. In your family you can be yourself.

Yet, on the other hand, family life can be the most fertile ground for tensions. The emotional stakes are so high that if expectations remain unfulfilled, disappointments may lead to a crisis or even to failure. Families are often overwhelmed by problems in school and at work. Unemployment and financial difficulties may threaten the sense of solidarity, and relationships may fall apart, even though such a relationship should provide support for financial problems or personal crises.

Another danger to our society is its growing individualization. Everybody wants to be strong and independent, as if he lived on his own island according to his own rules. Freedom and independence carried to such an extreme will keep people from standing up for one another. We cannot live together like that, for we will end up fighting one another. This is how even a home can turn into a place of constant conflict rather than a haven of peace, comfort, and understanding. Obviously, this leads to difficulties. In a relationship we need to feel responsibility for and loyalty to each other.

Considering this, I find it rather peculiar that many people value family life rather highly, yet seem to be incapable of committing to a relationship and taking on the responsibility of parenthood. I assume that growing egotism and past mistakes in their upbringing can explain this.

Our society runs the risk of becoming too single-minded. Individualism denies us the opportunity to relate to one another. From the very beginning to the very end, human life needs a community. The number of lonely and unhappy people is growing at an alarming rate. In larger cities the number of single-parent households has passed the fifty percent mark.

The Lack of Childcare

The lack of adequate childcare makes combining a family with a professional life even more difficult. Many women have to step back professionally if they want to have children. That may be a difficult decision. Recently one of my assistants, who had been with me for years, approached me with her predicament. She was pregnant, and, not having expected this at this stage of her life, she wasn't quite sure how to cope with a child and the demands of her career at the same time. I encouraged her, and told her what a gift children were. Children give a woman the chance to get to know a new life, to further develop their own sense of love and compassion. Children give a woman the opportunity to experience all facets of life: love, joy, happiness, and responsibility, yet also anxiety and disappointment. Children make life fuller and richer, so that a parent even finds him- or herself making sacrifices without a second thought. So we agreed that after her child was born, my assistant would come back to work part-time only. She has found that her daughter is most precious to her. When her daughter is older, she can come back to work for me full-time . . . if she wants to.

Every woman has to set her own priorities. The relationship between mother and child will benefit if the mother can stay at home with her child for the first three years. But I think our society should create more part-time jobs for young mothers, so that they can keep up with professional developments in their fields while they care for their children.

There are not enough kindergartens. Changing this will require private initiative. We cannot expect the government and churches to take care of this. Companies and citizens need to try and find solutions as well. For example, for many years now Bertelsmann has offered a company kindergarten and childcare in the "Villa Colorful." Between seven in the morning and five in the evening the children are lovingly cared for. They play, do gymnastics, and share their meals. Admission for a child is very much sought-after.

Any company carries social responsibilities, and more companies should offer such benefits to their employees. Many entrepreneurs and wealthy individuals seem to think that their responsibility toward society ends with paying taxes. This attitude reveals a troubling lack of responsibility and indifference towards social issues.

Another sore topic is all-day schooling. I don't think there are nearly enough all-day schools in Germany. I understand completely that the experiences of the Third Reich taught us to place the care and upbringing of our children in the hands of their parents rather than the government. Unfortunately, many parents don't take this responsibility seriously enough. Or perhaps they can't, because both parents work, or because they are single parents, or because they didn't learn how to do so in their own families. Our society has changed, and our political leadership needs to adapt our social structures to current demands and desires of the people.

I wouldn't make all-day schools the norm, but I'd offer them as a choice. I think all-day schools make more sense than sending children home alone after school, or worse, into the streets. Children left to their own devices suffer from a lack of guidance, and they may make bad choices or even engage in gang activities. All-day schools would help many families and worried parents. They'd know that their children have a warm dinner, and are supervised and kept busy with meaningful activities. Perhaps this could also take care of the touchy homework issue, which can put entire families under stress. Homework could be finished in the afternoon under the supervision of the teachers at school. I'm sure most families could do with one less difficult issue to deal with. I heard from the German Federal Parent Teacher Association that about eighty percent of parents are in favor of all-day schools.

We also need more flexible working hours and better conditions for part-time employees. Telecommuting will most likely be more common in the future, for it will allow women to keep working while caring for their children at home. Of course, this work situation bears its own disadvantages: Female colleagues have told me that you simply cannot program your children not to get fussy or disturb you while you are busy with important work. Another negative factor of telecommuting is the built-in threat of isolation. Men and women are social beings. We need to communicate with others as much as we need to breathe. Therefore many women prefer to go to an office to work, because the professional environment offers both distraction and inspiration. Be that as it may, professional women and mothers in part-time jobs are healthier and more content. Twenty-four percent of German non-working mothers, on the other hand, suffer from recurring depression.

If you ask any woman in a leadership position how they were able to combine work and family, the answer usually is, "You need the right man at your side. Only with her husband's support will a woman be able to grow."

I was fortunate enough to experience that firsthand.

6. My Role as Hostess and
My Role at Events

My professional responsibilities include hosting guests and representing the family at company functions. My husband appreciates my work as an important contribution to the public relations of our company. I enjoy being a hostess and bringing together people from different cultures and social fields. I love creating new contacts and having stimulating discussions about current problems and timely issues.

My work reminds my husband of his grandmother. He has such beautiful memories of Christmas with his family at his grandmother's house. Even at that time, before the war, they often invited guests. As my husband recalls, "It wasn't all that fancy—I mean to say that you couldn't serve dinner for twenty-five guests—but it was decorated nicely, with blue-and-white dishes, candles, and silverware. It was such a comfortable, yet elegant atmosphere."

There have been times when I've hosted about two thousand guests a year at my home. And to this day I hold numerous soirées. After an eight-hour conference at the Foundation, I run home to change and put on makeup and jewelry. In less than ten minutes (my housekeeper puts everything out for me) I am the smiling hostess greeting her guests happily, looking forward to their company.

Evenings at my home are especially popular. Our guests enjoy the casual feel of these get-togethers, because they can get acquainted on a more personal level. The next day a conference usually runs more smoothly and feels more pleasant. This is an important result of these evenings.

My guests often praise my talent for creating a tasteful

ambiance and a casual atmosphere. It took years to learn how to do that, because so many details come into play. The right lighting, such as candles and dimmed lights, can contribute to a good atmosphere. I enjoy trying out new ideas when I decorate my house for an evening. Usually I choose seasonal decorations. For years I've been working hand in hand with a few local florists. Let me share one example: In spring the lawn in front of my house blooms with yellow narcissus (It looks like a scene from *Doctor Zhivago*). So, in order to mirror my lawn, I have the florists turn my dining room table into a grass blanket full of colorful spring flowers. In summer we use different colored roses, because they go together well with the garden, and express the mood of the season. My guests are always thrilled. If an evening needs to be particularly elegant, I might even have orchids flowing from the chandelier down to the dining table. I did that when the Gorbachevs came to visit in 1992.

I get my ideas for decorations everywhere. My visual memory is quite good: I notice many details and store them in my memory like a movie. When needed, I just replay them. Flowers from all over the world, twigs, grass, ribbons, fruits, nuts, chestnuts, marbles—these days there is not a single thing you cannot use to decorate your home. I also find ideas at the fairs I visit regularly and in the international magazines on lifestyle, home, and garden I always read. I enjoy surprising my guests with new and fantastic ideas.

The menu depends on the season as well. You should never serve ingredients that smell strongly or are difficult to digest, such as onions, bell pepper, or garlic. And I know from my own experience that it is very important to have an aspirin handy and a needle and thread available. One of your guests might need them.

An attentive hostess will always entertain her guests. I like to have music to frame the evening: A pianist might play during the aperitif, and before dinner a young talent might sing opera or operetta pieces. It is my experience that music helps ease my guests into a casual mood after a tough day at a conference, and helps them to mingle and get to know each other.

I always give a ten- to fifteen-minute speech to greet the guests. The topic depends on the project and the participants of the evening. Usually I speak about culture, medicine, entrepreneurial culture, economics, or politics.

Sensitivity is very important when dealing with one's guests. I host international leaders, politicians, entrepreneurs, union leaders, scientists, artists, and other representatives of culture. My guest list has included: the former president of Germany, Roman Herzog; German chancellor Helmut Schmidt; the president of the Netherlands, Ruud Lubbers; Austrian chancellor Wolfgang Schüssel; Jürgen Strube, the chairman of the board of BASF; Hans Reischl, the chairman of the board of Rewe[1]; Klaus Zumwinkel, the chairman of the board of Deutsche Post AG[2]; the heart specialist Professor Reiner Körfer; as well as the stars Peter Maffay, Mireille Mathieu, Udo Jürgens and Peter Alexander.[3]

If the atmosphere is particularly good, we might spontaneously start singing songs. I don't think I sing all that well, but I enjoy it anyway. Once in a while I hand out the lyrics to a song—I might choose my Pathfinder favorite "Your Thoughts Are Free," for example. I've never met anyone who didn't like singing. On the contrary, sometimes my guests even ask, "Won't we sing a song tonight?" Well, then someone just starts. These evenings turn out splendidly, because music creates a sense of community.

I've invited a few prizewinners of our international singing competition, New Voices, to sing at the International Convention for Hospital Management. After they performed, I was trying to think of a song that everyone would know, so all of us—guests from America, Canada, Israel, South Africa, and Scandinavia—could sing together. I finally thought of "New York, New York," by Frank Sinatra. It worked—we all sang

---

[1] The *Rewe Handelsgruppe* is a German supermarket chain which has recently forayed into tourism as well.

[2] *Deutsche Post AG* is the German Mail Service, which only recently has been turned public.

[3] European stars of folk and pop music.

together. Between the verses someone would quickly give us the lyrics. We had a great time that evening. You can't plan something like that, you just have to improvise. That's probably why so many guests like it so much at my house.

But of course we don't just sing, we also have engaging discussions. I always make sure that nobody is bored and that everyone takes something home that evening. I try to look for a topic that is of interest to everyone, so I can avoid more than one conversation taking place at the same time. I'd rather engage every one of my guests in a single conversation. Small talk just isn't worth coming to Gütersloh for. Every single guest should take new thoughts and impulses home with him. That is another way of being polite and respectful towards one's guests.

I usually end the evening at around eleven o'clock. Many of my guests defer their nightcap to their hotel. The conference will continue the next day, and I want all my guests to be rested enough to participate. When my guests have left, I take a moment to relax with a glass of wine.

By the way, I usually host these events all by myself. This is the work division my husband and I agreed upon. My husband feels that I am especially talented at bringing people together, and so he leaves this up to me. He usually doesn't have enough time to participate anyway.

In the morning, I tell him all about the previous evening. My spirit soars when he acknowledges an evening's success. He says, "An endless number of people from all over the world get together here in Gütersloh. Our guests dive into a casual family atmosphere, they are served by my wife, greeted with one of her speeches, and serenaded by one of the singers from New Voices. The usual reaction is a sense of wonder among our guests that this kind of culture still exists. I am very glad that my wife has been able to maintain and develop this family tradition."

The Bertelsmann Foundation organizes so many conventions, symposia, and meetings for guests from all over the world that I felt the need to establish the company's own event service. When my guests feel comfortable, I feel beautifully compensated for all my hard work. I want every single room to look good during an event. No effort is too great to make sure that an evening turns out nicely. On mild summer days we hold our dinners and receptions outside, in the Foundation's courtyard.

In 1999 we organized fifty-six events with a total of 8,900 guests. Three of these events included more than 700 guests, and five of them included more than 200. We've also taken care of numerous conventions. By now, the Foundation's event department has twelve employees. It was my idea to grow and develop this department. The ladies wear dark blue suits and white blouses, tailored especially for these occasions. This way, our guests know who to turn to during our events. It signals to everyone that we are a team.

7. My Belief in People—
My Role Models

I have only positive feelings toward people. I believe that people are intrinsically good. This is another reflection of my attitude that a glass is half-full rather than half-empty. I have always been curious and open to new encounters, for I believe that the stranger I meet today may be my friend tomorrow. Because when you least expect it, you might find something valuable or endearing, something that corresponds to or adds to your own world of thought, in someone you didn't ever plan to meet. And perhaps you will even learn something. It is these special encounters you will always remember.

My first meeting with American professor Joel Fleishman was such an encounter. I had heard that he was a complicated and difficult person. I knew that he was a connoisseur of wines, so I invited him to my home for a seven-course dinner, paired with the appropriate wines and Champagnes. I know that in America it is polite to start a conversation with small talk, and so I asked him about his hobbies. I will never forget his beautiful answer. "Friends. I enjoy making friends and entertaining close relationships with them." Such a remarkable comment! Despite what I had heard, I learned he was a rather uncomplicated and helpful person. He became a close friend of the family.

I've found that I learn the most important things in life from other people, not from books. Five men and women have been especially important to me as my role models. First and foremost there is my mother, with her great love for people, her kindness, and her ever-positive outlook on life. Second is my husband with his vast knowledge and his impressive personality as a husband, a father, and an entrepreneur. He is my greatest teacher in all things concerning life.

Then there is the wife of a former general manager of our book club in Rheda. She's been like another mother to me. I will never forget when she stood before me for the first time. "My husband has told me so much about you, so I wanted to meet you personally. I wanted to know who you are and what you look like." That's what she said. It was the beginning of a true and deep friendship. Her name was Charlotte Borgmann. She was thirty years older than me and had no children. She was an independent woman of admirable character. I could talk to her about everything, even very personal and private things, and her advice helped me through many difficulties. She provided an anchor when things like childrearing, a large household, sick children, and my relationship with my husband threatened to become overwhelming to the young woman I was. Numerous times she told me I should have more patience, for if you look at things from a different angle, they prove to not even be half as bad as you thought. She provided a shoulder to cry on, and usually made me feel much better. But we also shared a lot of laughs. I admired her wisdom, and I learned so much from her: Patience, tolerance, understanding, and forgiveness. Her death ten years ago was a great loss for me.

The fourth person who's left an impression on my life is Teddy Kollek, the former mayor of Jerusalem. I met him about twenty years ago, when my husband and I visited Israel. He received us in his Spartan town hall offices near the old city walls. His office was full of papers, files, and books. Despite his rather forbidding demeanor, I realized that a good heart was beating beneath his rough exterior. He was so energetic and kind at the same time that he was able to inspire people. We quickly became close friends. We write to each other or get together when I am in Israel or any other chance we have. He is very straightforward and honest, and I like that about him. He says, "When I realize that something is right, then right it will be for me forever." Once he has made up his mind, he won't budge, and I think that's a rather positive characteristic. He has become very dear to me. Whenever I see him, or his wife, Tamar, all we do is look at each other and we understand each other perfectly. We have great respect for each other.

Teddy Kollek is pragmatic and has always wanted to achieve things that will serve the community, no more and no less. We have very similar thoughts and goals. A typical man of action, he loves to do things without discussing them to death in endless conferences. This is the kind of pragmatism that kept him in office for twenty years as the mayor of Jerusalem, to govern this difficult city that counts Arabs, Jews, and Christians, not to mention fanatics of all beliefs, among its citizens. He wanted to bring them all together, which is clearly the kind of work that turns a dream into yet another dream. His day would start at six in the morning, with three or four working breakfasts in a row. He would say, "Jerusalem is my life, and it will be until the end of my days." His work kept the peace in Jerusalem, not least because of his sensitivity toward the needs of all the different groups coexisting in the city. One example of his cultural sensitivity is a hospital department he built that makes it possible to treat Muslim men separately from Muslim women, because that is what the Islamic religion demands.

Once, after a conference we attended together, we strolled through town for a little while. He took me to the Arab part of town. I was quite surprised and impressed by the friendliness shown to him by Arabs and Jews alike. Everyone seemed to know him. This little scene speaks louder than any hymn of praise written about him. He is also very popular among American Jews, and he was able to collect a lot of money in America for his work in Israel.

I remember how my husband and I once read in the paper that fruit and tomatoes had been thrown at him in Jerusalem. We wrote an alarmed letter, asking him not to put himself into harm's way. We warned him that situations like this could be life-threatening. His answer was so simple. "If I need protection to

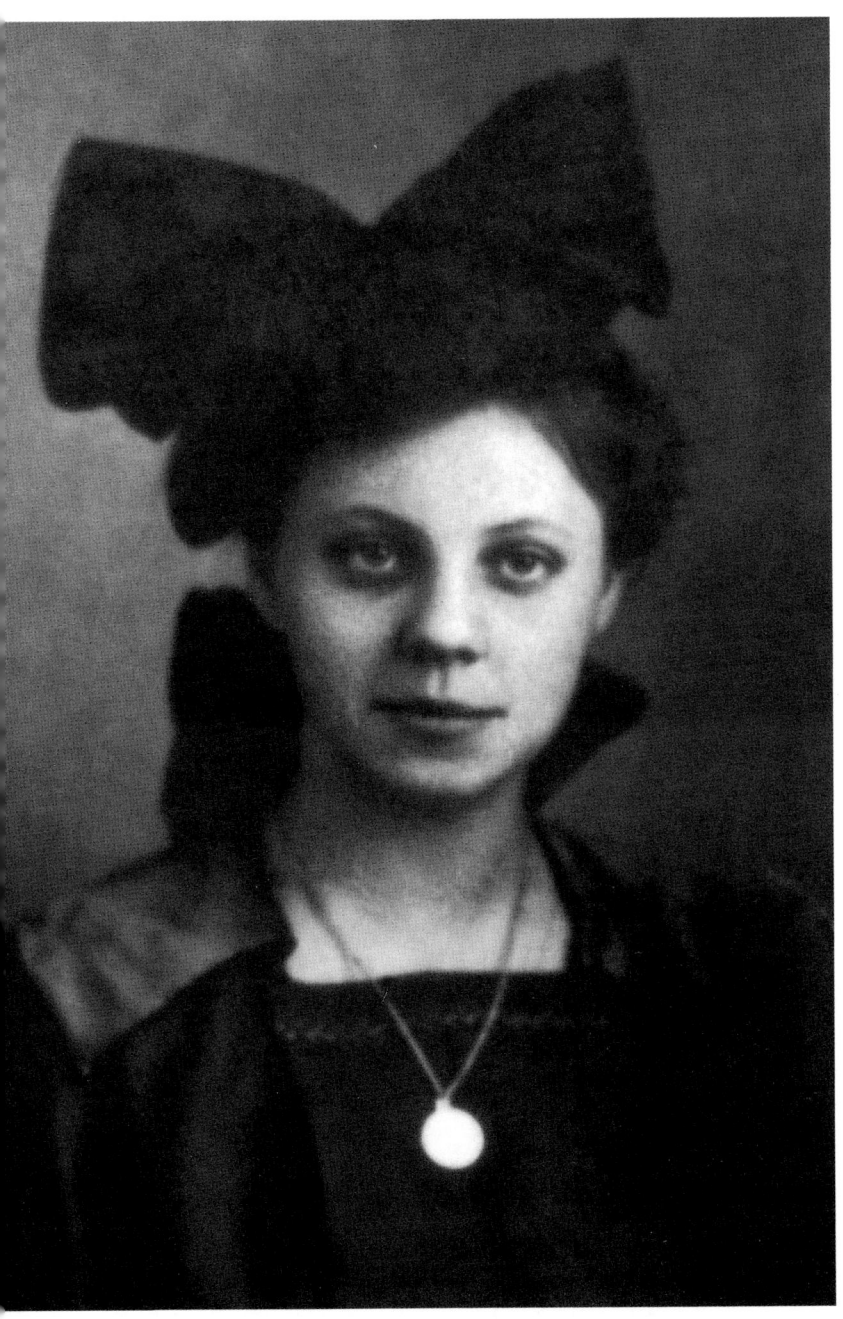

1 My mother, Josefa: To this day one of my most important role models.

2 The famous game of musical chairs—the first encounter and the beginning of a wonderful relationship with my husband.

3 My most precious possessions: my children Andreas, Brigitte, and Christoph, 1971, having fun in the water.

4 Pathfinders: Community and a sense of togetherness, responsibility and joy of life—here during a bicycle tour with my cousin.

5 On a great vacation on Rhodes in 1972.

6 Hats on: My best friend Jimmy A. Schmied and me at her daughter Alexandra's wedding.

7 A relaxed atmosphere during the fourth Kronberg Talk on Europe's Near Eastern and North African policies in 1998.

8 French singer Mireille Mathieu serenading my husband on his seventy-fifth birthday.

9 The great celebration of my husband's seventy-fifth birthday—Gütersloh, June 1996.

10 An atmosphere of change in East and West: the Gorbachevs visiting my home in Gütersloh in the spring of 1992.

11 A humorous speaker and popular guest: former German president Professor Roman Herzog at a symposium on foundation issues in April 1996.

12 Professor Everding and me congratulating the prize winners of the New Voices competition in 1997. In the center is Eteri Gvasava, who became an international star with the movie *La Traviata á Paris*.

13 The incomparable and unforgettable August Everding during the New Voices international competition in 1997.

14 Together with our friends entrepreneur Gerhard Weber and his wife Charlotte Weber-Dresselhaus at the final reception of the New Voices competition in 1995.

15 In the midst of the distinguished jury of the New Voices international competition in 1995: Hellmuth Matiasek, Kammersänger (a title awarded to the finest singers), Edda Moser, and director Ioan Holender from the State Opera in Vienna (from left).

16 Developing German-Jewish relations in a group that includes the former president of Israel Chaim Herzog (center) and the former German secretary of state Klaus Kinkel (right), in Bonn in 1997.

17 During a conversation on the Petersberg with Wolfgang Schäuble, Lord George Weidenfeld (center), and Professor Werner Weidenfeld during the German-Jewish dialogue in October 1997.

18 A good friend and an important partner during many projects like building the Mubarak Public Library: Suzanne Mubarak and myself during the inauguration of a branch of the library in Cairo in March 1999.

19 Handicapped by an arm injury: Mira Barak, wife of the President of Israel, during my trip to the Near East in Tel Aviv in 1999.

20 A charming and humorous conversationalist, an exceptional publisher and entrepreneur, and a good friend: the unforgettable Henri Nannen.

21 Enjoyable guests and pleasant conversationalists: Gerd Schulte-Hillen and Joel Fleishman.

22 Bringing together different fields of specialty: Monti Lüftner from the Bertelsmann Music Group and Professor Reiner Körfer of the Bad Oeynhausen Heart Center.

23 Thomas Middelhoff, chairman of the board of Bertelsmann AG, and myself, enjoying a reunion with Horst Teltschik, former general manager of the Bertelsmann Foundation, at the Frankfurt Book Fair in October 1999.

24 Building bridges between Israel and Germany: Teddy and Tamar Kollek, friends of ours for a long time, talking with the former governor of North-Rhine Westphalia, Johannes Rau.

25 An honest champion of tolerance and understanding: Ignaz Bubis visiting my home in 1998.

26 Hospitality from 1001 Nights: Sheikh Nahayan bin Mubarak Al Nahyan welcomes us in Abu Dhabi during our visit in March 2000.

27 An encounter on an important political level: with Jacques Delors, G. A. Yavlinskiy, Henry A. Kissinger, and Professor Werner Weidenfeld during a political discourse (from left).

28 The inauguration of the Friedrich List Monument in Warsaw with former U.S. secretary of state Henry A. Kissinger and former German president Dr. Richard von Weizsäcker in Warsaw.

29 An encounter with German chancellor Gerhard Schröder on the first Berlin Forum of the Bertelsmann Foundation in 1999.

30 Joel Fleishman during a conversation with my daughter Brigitte and me.

31 An audience with Queen Sophie during the awarding of the Prince of Asturia Prize to my husband in Madrid in October 1998.

32 The reception by the Spanish President José Maria Aznar López during the award of the Spanish Cross to my husband in Madrid in 1999.

33 Queen Noor of Jordan and myself during a gala dinner in 1998 in Berlin: the beginning of a beautiful and close friendship.

34 A royal visit at the "Planet m" of Bertelsmann AG on the EXPO grounds: my guests Queen Silvia of Sweden and Crown Princess Victoria in October 2000.

35 Conversations launching a mutual project "Keep children smiling in the New Millennium"—an international exchange program for our youth—with Jolanta Kwasniewska, the wife of the Polish President, in Warsaw in 1999.

36 Discussing the Eastern Expansion of the European Union with the Polish President Aleksander Kwasniewski (right) and participants of the IBF forum "Central and Eastern Europe en route to the European Union."

37 Among the participants of the forum "Central and Eastern Europe en route to the European Union" in June 1999 in Warsaw.

38 A valuable advisor and a good friend: The former President of the Netherlands and current UN commissioner for refugee issues, Ruud Lubbers.

39 A wanderer of continents and cultures, and a good friend: Lord George Weidenfeld during a conversation with my daughter Brigitte and myself.

40 An encounter with the recipient of the Nobel Peace Prize, Rigoberta Menchu, while presenting the report "Limits of Community" to the Club of Rome in Gütersloh in 1996. To the right: our friend of many years, partner, and advisor, Ricardo Diez Hochleitner.

41 Shared joy about German pop star Peter Maffay's donation of 150,000 Germany marks (U.S. $75,000) to the German Stroke Foundation after a concert in Halle/Westphalia in 1997.

42 Receiving a check for over 50,000 German marks (U.S. $25,000) for the German Stroke Foundation from the profit of the cookbook sale by the *Landfrauenverband Lette.*

43 German TV and movie star Uschi Glas. . . .

44 . . . and tennis star Boris Becker: My table partners during the celebration of the 60th birthday of magazine publisher Hubert Burda.

walk through my own town, I must have made a mistake some-where." And I will never forget what Teddy Kollek told me with regard to the multicultural life in Israel. "The problems we are having right now will catch up with Germany in a few years."

Finally, Roberto de Abreusodré has served as a role model for me. He was the governor of São Paulo, and then later Brazil's sec-retary of state. We met him through his son-in-law, a publisher, when my husband was creating the Bertelsmann Book Club in South America. His family is one of the wealthiest in the entire country. One weekend, Roberto invited us to visit one of his cof-fee farms. This farm was immense: It comprised about 100,000 acres, cared for by about two thousand employees. They all live in a village which reminded me of the backdrop of an American Western. Just imagine horses neighing and their hooves clomp-ing on the village streets, numerous small stores in a row, and only male voices to be heard in the saloon. We also went to visit his cattle farm. It was overwhelming: thousands of animals graz-ing on the meadows, cowboys riding their horses in their midst, swinging their lassos, and the endless horizon swallowing the red sun. Germany seemed so far away, and so very narrow and small in comparison.

We experienced a kind of hospitality I had never known be-fore. Thirty servants had come from São Paulo especially to care for us. Roberto had taken care of everything. When we arrived in our guest room we found hats to protect us from the sun and our suitcases unpacked. The next day our laundry had been washed, folded, and put away. Roberto made us feel wonderful. He seemed to say that there was nothing more important to him than spend-ing this time with us. His attentiveness wasn't only polite, it was full of warmth as well.

His wife, Anna Maria, told us amusing stories from her shop-ping trips to New York and Paris. She would take fifty empty suitcases. Upon her return the customs officers would ask her, "Where is the bus with the other guests?" She would laugh, "Which guests? These suitcases are all mine." I had only known this lifestyle from Hollywood movies. Servants in black suits and white gloves would serve us with champagne and caviar at the swimming pool. It was truly a different world.

Despite this rather extravagant lifestyle, Roberto is a humble man. One look into his big brown eyes will tell you that he is neither lofty nor unworldly. He knows the problems his country is grappling with quite well. He realizes the big chasm between rich and poor, and as a responsible person he worries about his country. His employees love him, and he has a good word for every one of them. He shows a lot of humanity and helpfulness. We were so close during that first visit, I felt as if I had known him all my life. My husband and I have a place in our hearts for him, always. When we left we were very moved. The thought that I might never see Roberto again brought tears to my eyes.

Deep down inside I knew I wanted to try and become a hostess as attentive as Roberto. I had learned so much from him in these few days. We became friends and have seen each other regularly ever since.

8. Encounters and
International Contacts

A frequent host is usually also a frequent guest. I receive so many invitations that give me an interesting glimpse into other worlds and cultures. Whether it is at my home or in royal palaces, during state visits, dinners, or receptions, I meet not only interesting but endearing and intelligent people who have an important contribution to make to our society.

Meeting the former German president Roman Herzog was an impressive encounter for me. The first time I met him was during a conference, when he and twenty other men were my dinner guests at my house. At the time he was still the president of the Federal Constitutional Court of Germany. He was seated at my table, and we got along splendidly. We agreed on many things, such as the importance of volunteer work and the significance of foundations in our society. I will never forget how warmly and openly he spoke of his relationship with his wife. He told me that they were real partners, that they would always stand up for each other, and that he would not make a single decision without first consulting his wife. His openness, honesty, and humanity made me think very highly of him that evening.

Later, after he had become president of Germany, we would meet more often, and it was then that I also got to know his wife, Christiane. I admired her for her dignity, the warm and caring commitment with which she represented our country, and for the great successes she achieves for the Mukoviszidose Foundation.

The three of us developed a rather friendly relationship with one another. On one occasion we talked about how important it is to take vitamins, particularly when under a lot of stress. I made a serious point of this to Roman Herzog. Later his wife told me that, in all their years together, she had never been able to make him take his vitamins, but I obviously had been able to convince him. Roman Herzog jokingly said, "I think about you every single morning, Mrs. Mohn."

I remember one sweet episode with the Herzogs on the day I was to receive the Charity Bambi[1] in Leipzig. I had planned to fly from Munich to Leipzig with a group of Bertelsmann managers. Our plane was already sitting on the runway when we were told we couldn't take off because of technical difficulties. Now what? Did we have to cancel the event? Looking out the window, I saw one of the military planes usually used by our politicians getting ready for take-off. Perhaps someone was in there who could help us? One of my managers and I raced over to the other plane. Security was guarding the escalator, but luckily, the body-guards recognized me and allowed me to board. On board were President Roman Herzog and his wife. Roman Herzog was surprised. "Mrs. Mohn, what are you doing here?" I told him about our predicament. As luck would have it, they were *en route* to Leipzig as well, because Christiane Herzog had been chosen to speak in my honor at the Charity *Bambi* awards. Of course they took me and my entourage along. The evening was saved.

An Official Visit to England

President Herzog's invitation to accompany him on an official visit to England in 1998 was a very special experience for me. Whenever he'd asked me to come along on one of his state visits as a representative of Bertelsmann and the Bertelsmann Foundation before, I'd had to decline due to other engagements. This time I was able to go.

---

[1] Originally, the *Bambi* was an acting award given for outstanding achievements in feature films and TV movies. Over the years, the *Bambi* has developed into an award given for excellence in areas including entertainment, fashion, beauty, sports, and charity. The recipients are chosen by popular vote.

My stay in England gave me a glimpse of what it is like to live like a queen. Riding a carriage to Windsor I experienced the curiosity and enthusiasm of the people cheering and waving to us along the way. I spent the night at Windsor Castle, which was once a Norman fortress, but which, over the centuries, had been remodeled as a Gothic castle. Its 680 rooms make it the largest occupied castle in the world, with about nine thousand employees taking care of the huge household. Needless to say, it was a grand experience to live in the house of the queen.

People say that Queen Elizabeth loves Windsor Castle. A few years ago, when the north wing burnt down, the queen was very upset. At the time she said, "Buckingham Palace is my office, but Windsor is my home." So it was decided to restore Windsor Castle, and the royal family paid two-thirds of the restoration cost of UK £110 million.

Every guest has to follow a specific protocol when visiting the queen. Even though every visitor receives clear instructions to that effect, President Herzog was somewhat confused. He said to me, "I have no idea when I am supposed to take off my top hat, and when I am supposed to put it on."

"Oh, don't worry, Mr. President," I said to him, "just watch Prince Philip, and do as he does!"

I had my problems with the etiquette as well. According to the instructions given to me, women were supposed to wear hats and white gloves at lunch. I love hats and enjoy wearing them, and I chose a black hat to go with my suit. I had just sat down at Princess Anne's table when I noticed that all the other ladies had already taken off their hats. I was the only one still wearing one! I had failed to take it off at the appropriate time, because I had been so engaged in a conversation. I got up quickly, stepped away from the table, and gave my hat to one of the queen's ladies-in-waiting.

The service at Windsor Castle was quiet and unobtrusive. When I got to my room, my suitcases had been unpacked. On my table I found the Royal Victorian Order, wrapped in blue velvet, which the queen had awarded me on this visit. Next to it was a booklet explaining when and how this order is to be worn. What an honor!

When I was getting ready for the procession and dinner at the castle, I found that my evening gown had been hung up in my wardrobe, but I couldn't find some of my other clothes. And so I called the chambermaid to ask her about them. She pointed to a chair upon which a piece of fine white English linen lay. On closer inspection I found that the linen was nicely covering my underwear. Everything I needed for the night had been set out for me. A truly royal service!

It is about a twenty-minute walk from the guest wing to the dinner rooms through empty hallways fully adorned with valuable masterpieces and antiquities. Windsor Castle is home to numerous selected paintings by van Dyck, Canaletto, and Holbein, among others. Walking through these long hallways I wondered how anyone can feel at home in such a huge and expansive building. I felt that it would be easy to get lonely in the midst of such splendor and greatness, because old walls and magnificent interiors cannot replace the warmth and attention of another human being. I believe that to live in such an environment, without intimacy and privacy, you have to grow up in it. Such a sacrifice requires an attitude which has to be practiced from an early age. My stay at Windsor Castle made that abundantly clear to me. I wonder whether true happiness is even possible in such a world.

I was introduced to the royal family during the procession in the Oak Room. According to protocol, it wasn't necessary to curtsy. The dinner took place in St. George's Hall, which is 200 feet long. The table was set magnificently: antique silver candlesticks, English roses everywhere, and silverware with the royal insignia. Music was playing in the background.

I was seated across the table from Queen Elizabeth, Princess Margaret, and the Queen Mother. Prince Andrew was at our table, and Prince Charles was nearby as well. I was able to watch the royal family "in action," and I realized how difficult it must be to behave royally. The royal code of behavior—remain calm and keep your composure under any circumstances, listen as if interested whether you are or not, and give an endless number of speeches about an endless list of topics—forces each and every member of the royal family to sacrifice a large part of his or her individual "self." I particularly liked the Queen Mother, who celebrated her hundredth birthday on August 4, 2000. She was quite impressive. She wore a champagne-colored lace dress, and on her head she wore a diadem, which must have been very heavy. She sipped Champagne with pleasure, chatted with animation and, over all, seemed very amused. I really admired her. But even for her an official dinner is a duty, something she's able to bear with a twinkle in her blue eyes. I talked to her about political and social life in England and Germany, about the relationship between our two countries, and about the future of Europe. I was impressed by her rich experiences. I suppose that once you are one hundred years old, you look at the troubles of our days with tranquility and wisdom.

I liked Princess Anne, too. She moved with a lot of self-confidence and sovereignty on the social floor, chatted charmingly with dignitaries, and was knowledgeable about international politics. You could tell that she's been moving in this world since childhood.

My encounter with the world of British tradition, and that of the royal family in particular, was rather impressive and interesting. Since then I have gained more insight into the British culture and the royal family. But I fear that the rigid fixation on the abundant rules and traditions hinders the country from keeping up with the times. My personal wish would be: Take one-third of the British formalities and transpose them to Germany. Less for them and more for us might strike the right balance.

Our trip to England was to be the last time I saw Christiane Herzog. I had known for a while that she was very ill. Her death affected me greatly. When I heard about her death, I couldn't help remembering what we had experienced together. She was a wonderful woman and will be greatly missed in Germany.

Encounters with Remarkable Personalities

Often I receive invitations for an evening not too far from Gütersloh, so I usually have my driver take me home at night. I'd rather get home at two in the morning than spend half the next day traveling, because then I can still keep professional engagements, even on a day after an evening out. If the drive takes several hours, I usually dress casually and comfortably in pants and a sweater, take my evening clothes along, and work in the car. Just before we get to my destination for the evening, my driver stops and I close the curtains of my limousine and change.

Recently Queen Beatrix of the Netherlands invited me to a dinner for twelve at her private palace in The Hague, *Huis ten Bosch* (in English, "House in the Forest"), a seventeenth-century residence with twenty rooms. It was the farewell dinner for the Israeli ambassador to the Netherlands, Avor Primor, who was to return to Israel. I knew him through the work we did together on several projects of the Bertelsmann Foundation and Bertelsmann AG in Israel, and I regard him highly.

I had brought along an evening gown with many small buttons. When, as usual, I was getting dressed in the car, five buttons came loose at the same time. It was a catastrophe! There was no way that I could show up to the royal dinner like that. For a moment I didn't know what to do, but then I had an idea. My driver Thomas Barnhöfer drove me to a large hotel in The Hague, where I told the reception desk personnel about my predicament. They were very understanding, since, after all, you can't go to a royal dinner with an open dress! An employee with needle and thread, along with a room in which to change, were offered to me immediately.

It turned out to be a very nice informal dinner with Queen Beatrix, her husband Prince Claus, Avor Primor, the German publisher Friede Springer, the Duke and Duchess Lambsdorff,[2]

[2] Otto Graf von Lambsdorff was the German economic minister from 1977–1984, and the leader of the liberal Free Democratic Party from 1988–1993.

and Otto von Gablentz, who was the former German Ambassador to the Netherlands.

This incident taught me to not only take an extra pair of stockings, and a needle and thread, but also an extra evening gown. And here's a tip for all of you ladies who are on the road as much as I am: Should you ever find yourself living the nightmare of finding a spot on your suit just as you are about to go to an official meeting, use the tissues you get on airplanes to administer "first aid." It's remarkable . . . they'll lift off any spot without a trace. I know, because it worked for me!

I enjoy looking back on my encounter with the Gorbachevs. I met them in the spring of 1992. Mikhail Gorbachev was in Germany to publish a book, and so we invited him and his wife to our home for an intimate dinner with only my husband, a few members of the board of Bertelsmann, and me. Mr. Gorbachev was very popular at the time, particularly in the West. It was the time of great transformation shortly after the Berlin Wall had come down. The Soviet Union found itself in a whirlpool of change, slowly moving forward on the path toward democracy, prompted greatly by Gorbachev's political efforts. The meeting was very warm and sincere. Mikhail Gorbachev took my hand in both of his, and it was as if we had known each other for a long time.

We were talking about the political and economic situation in Russia and about the implications of a future united Europe. He described vividly how heavy a burden it was to move his huge country toward the future, laden with patterns of thought that seemed stuck in the past. He was mostly worried that the road to democracy of the Soviet economy and society might detour, driving the country back into chaos. An interpreter was present to translate. I found Mikhail Gorbachev to be a very likeable man with incredible emotional strength, a sense of excitement, and *joie de vivre*. He mentioned that he would usually not go to bed before two or three in the morning because he needed all that time to get done what he had planned to do that day. He said, smiling, "Those who sleep too much will be punished in their lives."

His wife, Raisa, was a very intelligent woman with a strong feminine aura. She had studied sociology and politics, and obviously was an equal partner to her husband, supporting him fully in his visions of Russia. It was clear from the conversation how much they respected each other, for he would always consider her contributions. Her charm and her elegant appearance (with jewelry matching the color of her outfit) made Raisa Gorbachev a perfect match for her husband. Even I, as an outsider, could sense their intimacy: She was a part of him, and he was a part of her. They shared duty, joy, success, and failure, and clearly, they went through more than their share of it all. I assume that her health suffered from the psychological stresses in these times of transition and insecurity. My husband and I were moved immensely by Raisa Gorbachev's premature death.

Critics claim that Gorbachev made political mistakes, yet I find that he was a pioneer of our times by pointing both Russia and Europe toward a better future.

My husband and I are also friendly with Ruud Lubbers, the former chancellor of the Netherlands. He was one of the international leaders who participated in the International Bertelsmann Forum on the Petersberg in Bonn. I sat at a table with Helmut Kohl, who was chancellor of Germany at the time, the Spanish president Felipe Gonzales, and Ruud Lubbers. I remember this day well, because it was Helmut Kohl's birthday. Horst Teltschik, Helmut Kohl's advisor on foreign policies and, at the time, general manager of the Bertelsmann Foundation, had arranged for a birthday cake.

Ruud Lubbers knows the specific situation of entrepreneurs rather well, because he comes from a family of industrialists. So it was easy for us to find common interests. After his father's early death, Lubbers stepped up to his responsibilities and joined the board of directors of his late father's manufacturing company. He was so successful as an entrepreneur that two years later he became, together with his two brothers, one of three general managers of the company. His social and political commitment propelled him forward politically, and at only thirty-four he was appointed economic minister of his country, and at forty-three he was sworn in as the youngest chancellor his country had ever had.

His varied interests and vast experiences reminded me very much of my husband. Lubbers resigned as chancellor after twelve years. I wondered why, and whether the resignation hadn't been difficult, since, after all, a resignation also means a loss of influence, power, contacts, and lifestyle. He answered that he had been on the political stage long enough, and that he didn't want to be in office as long as Helmut Kohl. He firmly believed that he had lived an intensive life during his years as chancellor of the Netherlands, and that it was time to pass that responsibility on to other competent hands. His relaxed attitude impressed me very much. Then as much as now he is a popular guest of the Bertelsmann Foundation, and his advice and knowledge are always very much appreciated.

Ruud Lubbers played a major role in creating the Foundation of Work in the Netherlands, an institution whose purpose is to mediate between unions and entrepreneurs on tariffs and social issues. My husband, myself and the committee of the Bertelsmann Foundation were so impressed by the institute's work that it was awarded the Carl Bertelsmann Prize in 1997.

Today Ruud Lubbers teaches at several universities and works for the Club of Rome, where I am a regular member and my husband is an honorary member. This is how we keep in regular contact and were able to build a warm friendship.

Ruud Lubbers will became the UN Commissioner for Refugee Issues in 2001. I am very happy for him, not only because I am convinced that he will do exceptional work, but also because it recognizes his achievements in fostering a healthy balance and understanding between people and cultures.

Another good friend is the English publisher Lord George Weidenfeld. He was born in Vienna, where he spent his youth until Hitler's annexation of Austria forced him to escape to England after the Germans seized his father. Weidenfeld worked as a journalist during the war, and then started a publishing house in London, where he lives to this day. For the past twenty-four years he's been a Life Peer,[3] yet his political activities have remained limited to speeches informing the Upper House of Parliament about the politics of Israel. He's never held political office. We've known him for many years, and once he even took me to a luncheon at the House of Lords. I'll never forget the celebration of his eightieth birthday, which friends organized at Trinity House. I was fascinated by the elegance of the affair: The furniture was as valuable as museum pieces, decorated with exquisite roses and hortensias, pink velvet bands, and velvet tablecloths, illuminated elegantly with candles in silver candlesticks. It looked fantastic. Lord Weidenfeld sat next to me. He is still a ladies' man, charming, entertaining; a gentleman you rarely find today. In short, he is very British. Small wonder that all the speakers that evening were women!

He actively supports the German-Jewish dialogue initiated by the Bertelsmann Foundation, and, like me, he is a member of the Salzburg Academy of Sciences. His contacts around the world (and the fact that he shares them willingly) are priceless.

Lord Weidenfeld initiated the Club of Three, of which I have been a member from the very beginning. The basic idea is that Great Britain, France, and Germany not only have to grow closer politically and economicaly, but also need to understand, tolerate, and overcome their differences in order to progress on the way to a unified Europe. Regular meetings among pundits and decision makers in areas such as politics, the economy, the sciences, and the media are meant to support this development. We met for the first time in June 1998 at Lord Rothschild's Spencer House in London, and again in December 1999 in Berlin, both at the house of the Deutsche Bank as well as Unter den Linden at the DaimlerChrysler Corporation. Our speakers have been, among others, the Governor of Saxony, Kurt Biedenkopf, the German president Johannes Rau, and various economic managers such as Klaus Mangold and Rolf E. Breuer, both members of

[3] A British honorary title.

the board of directors of DaimlerChryser. The Club is a forum for stimulating discussions that are meant to share innovative ideas, to make new contacts, and to find common goals among the participants.

My husband and I are also good friends with the Spanish publisher Ricardo Diez Hochleitner, who has been president of the Club of Rome since 1991. We met him many years ago through mutual acquaintances in the publishing world. Diez Hochleitner is a very educated man who studied economics in Spain and chemistry at the Technical University in Karlsruhe, Germany. He was a professor in Spain and Colombia, and then held numerous positions in the field of education at UNESCO and the OAS. Today Diez Hochleitner mostly works in publishing as the vice president of the Spanish media group Timon, as well as in the Santilla Foundation and as a member of the administrative board of the PRISA (the daily newspaper *El País*).

The three of us (my husband, myself and Diez Hochleitner) have initiated a cultural dialogue. We have come to admire his worldly manner, his vast knowledge, and his charming behavior toward others. He is a very pleasant conversationalist on any and all current topics. He listens calmly and intently before he shares his opinion or, if requested, his advice. Ricardo Diez Hochleitner joined the committee of the Bertelsmann Foundation in 1993, and has been a regular guest and advisor ever since.

Numerous magazines, publishing houses, music companies, a printing company, and even a book club have represented our company in Spain for thirty-five years. The *Círculo de lectores* takes on a different, much more important role in Spain than the Bertelsmann Book Club does in Germany. The club counts 1.5 million members, among them the king himself, and it has sold 200 million books. It is a cultural institution the Spanish are very proud of.

In 1995 my husband founded the *Foundación Bertelsmann* in Barcelona with the express purpose of nurturing and fostering general reading and media culture, as well as the development of public libraries and the educational support of future leaders. Jury president Manuel Olivencia said, "Through the building of several libraries and the publication of millions of books and other reading materials, Mohn and his company have made a worthwhile contribution to the literary culture in Spain." Olivencia also praised my husband's entrepreneurial model of employee participation in company decisions. My husband received an award from Crown Prince Felipe in the Theater of Oviedo in northern Spain. Even Queen Sofia was present.

My husband received the Prince of Asturia Prize, one of the highest awards of Spain. The jury selected him in the fields of communication and liberal arts "for incomparable life achievement." In addition, my husband received the Great Cross for Civil Service from President José María Aznar in 1999, as a token of appreciation from the Spanish government for my husband's entrepreneurial achievements, which have placed the fostering of cultural values in Europe and the world over at the center of his life's work. Afterward my husband and I were received by the Spanish king Juan Carlos in the Zarzuela Palace in Madrid.

We've admired the Spanish royal family for many years. They are very modern, uncomplicated, informal, and behave almost like commoners. They are exemplary representatives of their country. My husband and I particularly like Crown Prince Felipe, because he is a very cultivated and likeable young man, someone who gives a mature and grounded impression. Spain can be proud of King Juan Carlos and Crown Prince Felipe, who will eventually follow in the king's footsteps. It helps a country tremendously if its leaders provide continuity.

When recently my husband's book, *Humanity Wins*, was introduced in Spain, Crown Prince Felipe remarked to my husband with a laugh, "Your book is so full of knowledge and experience that I will put it under my pillow so I can understand it more quickly."

I met Bill Clinton with a mixture of curiosity and apprehension. After all, there were all those scandals around him. We were introduced at a state reception in Berlin, where he was chatting with Roman Herzog and Helmut Kohl. He gave me an endearing smile. "So, you are Mrs. Bertelsmann." I was surprised that he was so well-informed and even knew of Bertelsmann's newest acquisition, Random House in New York. I was told that he takes notes on people he finds interesting. I noticed his youthful charm and his twinkling blue eyes. Afterward I told my husband, "I can relate to every woman who would like, just once, to have dinner with him."

Cultural Projects all over the World

Often a friendly personal contact marks the beginning of a mutual project. One example is my encounter with Suzanne Mubarak, the wife of the Egyptian president. When we met, we liked each other immediately and have remained friends ever since. She is a warm and productive person, who takes care of the cultural and educational issues in her country. Through our personal relationship, the three of us (Suzanne Mubarak, my husband, and I) have been able to bring our two cultures closer to each other.

Mrs. Mubarak and I got to know each other during our work building a public library in Cairo, for which the Bertelsmann Foundation financed marketing and management. Suzanne Mubarak uses all her knowledge and intelligence to fight for her country like a mother. She possesses an intelligence that springs not only from formal knowledge, but also from experience and humanity. That's what we like so much about her. The library was an Egyptian initiative, and was first mentioned to us during a conference called "The Mediterranean Challenge—the European Answer." Political leaders and cultural representatives from African and European countries bordering the Mediterranean participated in this conference. An Egyptian participant approached my husband and asked whether he would be interested in showing commitment to Muslims rather than only to the Jews in Israel. My husband answered, "Sure, why not?" As an international media empire, our purpose is always to support and foster reading and education all over the world.

When the Egyptian ambassador came to visit us in Gütersloh to discuss the conditions of the library we envisioned, my husband carefully asked how much the library would be used, as he understood that about fifty percent of Egyptians were illiterate. The ambassador corrected my husband, saying that about sixty percent of Egyptians didn't know how to read. This was all the more reason for us to continue with this project, because my husband and I liked the idea of supporting a literacy program in Egypt. Reading provides education. Reading can be the first step out of the hopelessness of poverty and into the ability to make your own livelihood. When you know how to read and do math, you can become a merchant, or find other employment with which to support yourself and your family. Literacy can help the beggar off the streets. Teaching people to help themselves is the most meaningful form of help I can imagine.

The Egyptian government gave us President Nasser's old villa, a beautiful place right down by the river Nile, and the Bertelsmann Foundation paid the remodeling costs. The opening of the Mubarak Library two years ago in Cairo was a grand event. I remember the strict security protocol we all had to follow. Purses, bags, everything was checked minutely. To illustrate: I was waiting for Mrs. Mubarak with two of my collleagues, who had accompanied me to the event and whom I wanted to introduce to Mrs. Mubarak. When she finally arrived and I greeted her, security officers led the two other ladies into another room. This made it apparent that Mr. and Mrs. Mubarak live under a constant security protocol intended to minimize the risk to their lives. Apparently everything, including their meals, is prepared separately. During the opening there was even a special bathroom for the two of them, which was closed off to all other guests. I really admire them for their commitment to their country despite the obvious risk to life and limb.

Since its opening, the library has become a lively cultural center, used so heavily by the population that people wait in line for a long time to get in. Numerous performances take place in the well-tended garden, some even by and for children, and whenever there is a state visit in Cairo, the library is part of the official program.

This reminds me of a touching fact: During an official visit, the library is decorated with truckloads of flowers. Once the official visitor has left the library, the flowers are loaded onto the trucks and brought to the next stop. If one of the plants is left behind by accident, the library employees are sheepishly happy, because it means they can keep it for good.

Not too long ago I participated in the opening ceremony of a second library branch in a very poor section of Cairo. The people there are the poorest of the poor . . . they are barefoot and own nothing but the clothes on their backs. I think it's good to open a branch there, so that even these people have a chance at a decent education. There was a lot of security during this opening as well. My personal assistant had not been registered as a guest, and so I claimed that he was my bodyguard to get him in anyway. It seemed like a believable cover, and I think that little white lies are allowed once in a while.

I've heard since then that the library has been rather popular. Children and teenagers stand in long lines in order to be let in. In my opinion it is our duty as a media empire to help in that way. I'm especially glad to report that our initiative seems to have fallen on fruitful ground. The individual mayors of the other parts of town have started establishing their own libraries with the help of local businesses and industries. It's a small step on the arduous road to reducing illiteracy in Egypt.

Mrs. Mubarak and I have a new plan already. Considering that the international singing competition, New Voices, has become an important part of our foreign cultural policies, Mrs. Mubarak and I came up with the idea to initiate and organize regular cultural events around the competition. These events are meant to foster international understanding above and beyond national, cultural, and religious borders.

For example, in Spring 2001, we want to offer a master course with twelve vocalists in Cairo. In addition, we want to bring together about forty representatives of politics, education, the sciences, the economy, and the media to open a cultural dialogue on current issues. Such a symposium would be an excellent opportunity for two cultures to find a common ground and common goals. The topic for Cairo is "Arabic and European Identity: The Dialogue of Two Cultures." The evening concert the young artists of the master course will perform will be the grand finale of the event. We believe that this will offer sincere cultural exchange on the one hand, and nurture new talent on the other. The Bertelsmann Foundation is planning similar events in Japan, China, and other countries.

It is so nice that I've been able to develop so many international contacts, for personal connections make it possible to get many projects underway without having to deal with red tape. That's why some people have given me the unofficial title of Cultural Ambassador. It is always fascinated me that, although people are from different cultures, they can still share feelings which span borders.

This was my experience with Jolanta Kwasniewska, the wife of Polish president Aleksander Kwasniewski. She invited me for tea during the International Bertelsmann Forum in the Warsaw Presidential Palace in 1999. We were pleasantly chatting for about two hours, and I was surprised at how self-confident and sovereign she seemed to be in her role as Poland's first lady. Her commitment to fight poverty in her country is admirable, and so I offered my advice on starting foundation work, based on my experiences with the Bertelsmann Foundation. She invited me to participate in the 1999 conference "Keep Children Smiling in the New Millennium," a collaboration of several countries meant to improve the future of children and increase understanding among the peoples of the world. Four queens and fifteen wives of presidents participated. My meeting with Jolanta Kwasniewska started the project, Schools of Tolerance, which will send teenagers between the ages of fifteen and seventeen from different nations to a summer camp with teenagers from Bosnia and

Herzegovina. The first camp is planned for the year 2001 in Poland. The main idea is to familiarize the children with the differences among peoples and to foster tolerance through discussions as well as through youth-oriented activities. This is intended to help these teenagers realize the common ground that they share which connects rather than separates people above and beyond cultural, ethnic, and social differences. We hope that the initiative will contribute to peace and mutual understanding between the peoples of the world. I think this is a good idea and the right thing to do, and I will make sure that two teenagers from Germany will participate.

In May 2000 I met Queen Silvia of Sweden for lunch in Munich. We had met the year before at the "Keep Children Smiling" conference in Warsaw. She contacted me through an old schoolmate of mine, Achim Middelschulte, chairman of the board at Ruhrgas AG[4], because she wanted me to participate in the World Childhood Foundation, which helps neglected, impoverished, orphaned, and abused children by improving the conditions for life worldwide. Every single child should have a fair chance at happiness. The foundation wants to improve the situation of the ten million children living on the streets worldwide, as well as aggressively search for missing children. In addition, the foundation offers an intensive educational program against sexual abuse and child pornography, as well as against drug abuse and criminal activities involving children and teenagers. Finally, the foundation supports educational efforts that will create a better future for our children. Headquartered in Sweden, the foundation supports projects in Brazil, Africa, and Latvia.

Queen Silvia, some of her German friends, my personal assistant, and I had a very intensive and fruitul conversation about her and my foundation work, during which she also expressed great concern for health issues. The meeting was very informal and warm. Queen Silvia is very charming, a real lady with a lot

---

[4] *Ruhrgas AG* is a German gas company headquartered in Essen.

of style and dignity. She was listening very attentively, while maintaining eye contact. I find that very important, because I don't like it at all when people let their eyes wander while they speak with you. I promised my support of the queen's World Childhood Foundation and agreed to do the media work for her foundation in Germany.

I also have a very friendly relationship to Queen Noor of Jordan. I met her in Berlin in 1998 during an event of the UWC (United World Colleges), shortly after her husband's death. We were sitting next to each other at the table, and we took to each other immediately, as if we were on the same emotional wavelength. Even though we haven't known each other for very long, we can talk about personal things. We chatted for about four hours that first evening, about everything, including her late husband King Hussein. She revealed how painful his death was for her, especially because she misses talking with him. I could relate to that. She confided that she felt obligated to keep working in the service of her country in accordance with her husband's wishes, and that she felt that he was always with her. I could relate to that as well. Our beliefs are very similar. I would do the same thing, work and live in accordance with my husband's wishes. For, after all, a wife carries on the responsibility even after her husband's death.

She was telling me about her foundation which works toward peace in the Middle East and the further development of Jordan. After mentioning my work at the Bertelsmann Foundation and Bertelsmann AG, we discussed whether the Bertelsmann Foundation might get involved in Jordan. She invited me to visit Amman so she could show me her country. We hugged each other warmly when we said good-bye.

Encounters like that are like a gift, because it is rare that two people who've just met feel so close and get along so well. It has little to do with one's social status, but a lot with thinking and feeling alike. It's so very beautiful, and I am very grateful for that.

While on a trip through four countries six months later, I visited Queen Noor in Amman. My husband and I had just visited

Egypt and Israel, where we took part in a meeting of the board of the Mubarak Library in Cairo, and, later, in a meeting of the board of the Adam Institute in Jerusalem, an exemplary institution focused on education toward tolerance and democracy. Of course, we scheduled several conversations and dialogues, among others with our old friend Teddy Kollek. Then we separated, my husband flying back to Gütersloh, and I continuing on to Jordan and Abu Dhabi.

The short twenty-minute flight from Jerusalem to Amman brought home to me how geographically close Jordan and Israel are. It was my first trip to Amman, and I was pleasantly surprised by the landscaping along the streets from the airport to the downtown areas. I hadn't expected green trees and roses in a desert country. Of course the plants and trees are made possible by irrigation only. I was also surprised at the number of new houses and streets in town.

I had just arrived at my hotel when the phone in my room rang. I was sure it was one of my colleagues who had accompanied me, but, much to my surprise, it was Queen Noor calling to make sure that I had arrived safely and found everything to my satisfaction. Her inobtrusive attentiveness was so very pleasant and endearing.

In the evening Queen Noor and one of her foundation's directors, one of my personal assistants, and I were to dine together in her palace. The long drive to the palace, picturesquely located above the city, takes you past green lawns, again made possible by careful irrigation. There were several security checks before we reached the palace. Two stone lions stood guard at the portal which opened by itself. In the center of the large foyer was a grand piano with family pictures framed in silver. The room seemed almost like a chapel, including the calming effect it had on me. I signed into the large guest book.

From the foyer we went into a salon, which captivated me with its brown terracotta tones. I particularly liked the floor, tiled with brown travertine, which is a limestone from quarries around Rome, found in every Roman palace. Queen Noor entered, wearing a blue dress which beautifully complemented her blond hair and her big blue eyes. She has a very warm charisma, and her majestic stature fills an entire room.

We ate next door in the small oak-panelled library. The table was nicely set. Queen Noor mentioned that the plates were painted by employees of her foundation. Talking about potential projects we could work on together, we agreed that tolerance education is greatly important not only in Jordan, but also in Europe. I came up with the idea of organizing a youth exchange program between Germany and Jordan. Young Jordanians would work in our company and could see not only how we work and live, but also what our family life, religion, and culture are like. And, vice versa, Germans would travel to Jordan. This, we hope, would help our countries to get to know each other better and to build bridges of mutual understanding.

Industrialized nations have the moral duty to help poorer nations. Poverty and hunger in underdeveloped countries create hatred and war, and we want and need to avoid that at all cost. Perhaps in time Jordanian institutions may participate in the network of the Israeli Adam Institute, an opportunity for an exchange between the Israeli and Jordanian youth.

The next day we visited the House of Arts, a project created by Queen Noor's foundation where women learn to do crafts like sewing, embroidering, pottery making, and carpet weaving. Their work is for sale, and I bought four very nice carpets which I put into the guest rooms in my house in Gütersloh.

I was most impressed, however, with the way this project fosters tolerance and conflict resolution among children and teenagers. We attended a performance of a scene from a musical put together by teenagers for school-age children. The scene portrayed a conflict between two young people, who were fighting loudly. On the puppet stage behind them, puppets commented on what was going on, asked why the children were fighting, and gave instructions as to how to resolve the confict in a better way than with fighting. The actors tour schools and theaters with this thought-provoking performance. It is important to teach children tolerance and conflict resolution, for it may help stop the development of stereotypes and prejudices.

I said good-bye to Queen Noor with the promise that I would work with her on projects with the express goal of developing tolerance.

I continued on to Abu Dhabi, because Sheik Nahayan bin Mubarak al Nahyan had invited me to come visit his country. I had met him in Gütersloh through Arvato, the technical side of Bertelsmann, which at the time was bidding for the prestigious project of printing the Koran in Arabic. The forty-four-year-old Sheik is considered to be a Western man, perhaps because he studied at Oxford. Be that as it may, he is also the cultural minister of his country. He came to Gütersloh because, in addition to his interest in the Bertelsmann products in general, he was planning to build a library in Abu Dhabi, and he wanted to visit the Gütersloh city library. This library was built by the Bertelsmann Foundation and the city of Gütersloh as a pilot project with pioneering ideas on organization, equipment, and finances. It is not just a place of books, but also a meeting place for all the citizens of Gütersloh, and an up-to-date informational center offering classical and state-of-the-art media. It is meant to be a library for citizens of all backgrounds, not only bookworms and those already interested in culture.

The Sheik was impressed by this concept. Instead of the master library he had originally planned, he now wanted our support to create his own "center of knowledge." His idea was to create a prestigious project with a state-of-the-art Internet connection and a link to all the universities of his country. Sheik Nahayan is very committed to fostering education and economic innovation in his country so that it can keep up with the developments in the twenty-first century. He wants every citizen in his country to have a computer. My husband has always praised the fact that this is a very meaningful use of the billions of dollars of oil money in the country, particularly considering that there may be a time when the oil will dry up. The Sheik's farsighted policies center on his active role in fostering educational policies. Attempting to attract know-how from all over the world, he invites the best professors to teach at his universities, where they work with small groups of no more than fifteen students. Compared to our over-stuffed lecture halls in Germany, the students there learn, and the teachers teach, under much better conditions. It is remark-able that about 60 percent of women study at women's universi-ties.

When we first met in Gütersloh we told the Sheik about our family traditions and about the 160-year-old tradition of the house of Bertelsmann. He seemed particularly interested in the company's special culture. It is this personal contact that will cre-ate trust and loyalty necessary to do business with our Arabic partners.

This is why I was treated like a state visitor when I traveled to Abu Dhabi. It was a trip into a different and fascinating world. The skyline you see when flying in looks as if someone had trans-planted the skyscrapers of New York into the desert. And the landscaping, with an abundance of greenery and flowers all around, a legacy of the Sheik's father and taken care of by Pakistani foreign workers, is overwhelming. I don't want to know how much water is used just for that.

I was introduced to the other dinner guests, ministers, and dig-nitaries of the country during an interesting ceremony. As the honorary guest I was sitting at the head of the table next to the Sheik. The other guests were introduced one by one, each then taking a seat to the right and left of the table. Arabic manners prescribe standing during somebody's introduction, and so we were constantly getting up and sitting down and getting up and . . . considering that there were 150 dinner guests, you can imagine how long this ceremony lasted. Huge bowls with saffron rice and meat were presented on dark wooden tables, which were heavily decorated with flowers. They served lamb, and in my honor (as is customary for special guests) they also served the meat of a seven-day-old camel. Within the humps, which are very fatty on top, hides excellent meat. The Sheik gave me the best pieces. Some people might decline foreign tastes like that, but I like to try everything while I am traveling. I found the camel's meat to be very tasty. By the way, the Arabs, including the Sheik, were eating with their hands, as is customary in Arabic countries, but the Westerners were given knives and forks to eat with. Of course, there was no alcohol. When approaching us the servants bowed. And here's an interesting little cultural tidbit: When drinking the sweet Arabic coffee, shaking your cup means that you don't want any more coffee, holding it still means you do.

I was given a very interesting glimpse into a vastly different culture, and met open and warm people. I felt enriched by this trip, because such encounters give you important experiences to help you understand and value foreign customs and rituals.

Since Sheik Nahayan was very interested in the Bertelsmann corporate culture, he later invited my husband to give a lecture on the topic in Abu Dhabi. So I got to travel to the country a second time.

Once again we were warmly welcomed. Sheik Nahayan came to pick us up from our hotel suite personally, which, as is typical for the Arabic style, glittered with gold. In honor of his guests our host was wearing a white robe with golden embroidery. He was a very attentive host, and I couldn't help feeling like a state guest. This time, though, it was my husband who was the honorary guest, not me. His lecture on the Bertelsmann culture was received with great interest, and the Sheik was impressed by the company's 160-year-old family tradition. It spells continuity, trustworthiness, and integrity, and it is the basis for our business relations and the mutual friendships we maintain with the cultures with which we do business.

The next day the Sheik wanted to show us his private island, so we took his private jet to one of the fifty-six islands that comprise Abu Dhabi. The plant and animal life in the middle of a desert country seemed like a mirage. There were millions of palms, bushes, and trees, as well as colorful and exotic flowers. About sixty thousand animals such as goats, ostriches, antelopes, giraffes, flamingos, peacocks and numerous other birds populated the island. In between were small artificial ponds, so the animals would have enough to drink. The summer palace of the Sheik's family is located in the center of the island, and, with its light turquoise color, looks as if it grows out of the green of its surroundings like a dream from *1,001 Arabian Nights*.

The dialogue with the Sheik was pleasant, guided by the mutual respect for each other's culture and traditions. I believe that this mutual attitude helped our cooperation nicely. I'm good at taking care of our investor relations, and I'm very happy that I can contribute to the success of a project in that way. My husband and I are very grateful for the valuable dialogue and cooperation with Sheik Nahayan and his employees.

9. Medical Projects

When Darkness Falls

How colorful the world is when you can see! Mother Nature creates a harmony of abundant colors, such as beautiful sunrises and sunsets, mountain panoramas, the colorful play of the ocean, and the splendid display of all the colors of plant life. Most of us take the ability to see for granted, but so many, those with uveitis for example, can't see any more. What is uveitis?

Uveitis is a recurrent inflammation of the vascular tunic of the eye, which can befall even children and teenagers. Uveitis may result in permanent damage to your eyesight, and can, in some cases, even lead to blindness. This illness can be a huge physical and psychological burden both for those affected and their loved ones. Uveitis sufferers may have to deal with a very sudden onset of this illness, and may experience a period of torturous uncertainty with unanswerable questions and immeasurable pain. Often they embark on an odyssey leading from one doctor to the next, because neither diagnosis nor therapy of this disease is that well known. In about 90 percent of the cases the causes for the disease remain unknown. The illness may be a one-time event, or it may be chronic. The latter can lead to retinal detachment and, ultimately, to blindness.

Our youngest son Andreas fell ill with uveitis at the age of seven. Quite frankly, we discovered the illness more or less by accident. At the time, the four-year-old daughter of a friend of mine had been diagnosed with cancer of the eye. This tragic diagnosis of my friend's daughter inspired me to ask our nanny to take the children to the ophthalmologist immediately for a checkup. To this day I believe that this haphazard decision was somehow meant to be. The eye specialist asked me to call him personally at once. And so I found out that our youngest son had uveitis. What a shock!

Our family wasn't familiar with this illness or with its implications. Quite frankly, we didn't even know its name. We were desperate, and looked for information on causes and possible treatments for this illness everywhere. Our son embarked upon a long and arduous road of suffering, with frequent headaches and immeasurable pain in his eye. During acute phases he wouldn't be able to see and thus missed school. Frequently he wouldn't even be able to play like the other kids. It was so painful for everyone to see him suffering like that. All of us lived in fear for him and his eyesight, a fear that tortured me night and day. We were searching the world for specialists, and finally found them close to home, in Europe, at the univerity hospitals in Zürich and Kiel. Professor Boeke from the university hospital in Kiel explained to us that uveitis has many phases, but few treatment options. Since the causes of the disease usually remain unclear, the center of any treatment plan must be the symptoms. The cause, however, remains unknown. Usually the symptoms can be kept under control with cortisone treatment, yet we decided not to rely on this alone, and also turned to alternative treatments such as acupuncture and homeopathic medicine.

Two years after the diagnosis we were vacationing in the Seychelles. In addition to uveitis, our son was also afflicted by neurodermitis on his feet, which we usually treated with cortisone. While vacationing I noticed that his neurodermitis had disappeared after about two or three days, even though we had not used any of our cortisone creams at all. After we returned home our ophthalmologist noticed that his eyesight had improved as well. We felt surprise and joy at the same time. How had this happened?

Since both his eyes and his skin had improved at the same rate, the doctors thought that both illnesses might have been influenced by the same treatment. The question now was whether it was the ocean air, the temperature, or the intensive light that had caused the improvement. The doctors tried to sort this out, for if our son's condition had improved so much during our stay in the Seychelles, a climate or light therapy might be able to help other patients as well.

This was reason enough for me to initiate a uveitis research project at the Foundation. It became an affair of the heart to help people who are afflicted with this disease. There are about 200,000 uveitis sufferers in Germany, and the cost of treatment is estimated at about 300 million German marks (US $150 million) per year.

The Bertelsmann Foundation supported pilot studies at the university eye clinics of Kiel and Münster in search of data supporting my observations. The first experiment was an all-expenses-paid, three-week stay on the Dead Sea in Israel for eighty patients under medical supervision. Forty-four percent of the patients showed improvement, with some of the patients experienceing a total recovery. The other patients experienced fewer acute phases, or acute phases that wouldn't last as long or were less intensive. Many patients needed less, or even no, cortisone. The studies had proven that the healing process of this disease was influenced by light and climate.

Light and climate therapy strengthens the immune system by virtue of intensive ultraviolet radiation from the sun. Because the Dead Sea lies far below sea level, the positive UVA radiation is strong, while the dangerous UVB radiation is filtered out. So it is possible to sunbathe for a long time without getting sunburned. The therapy is meant to be a whole-body treatment with as little clothing as possible, so that large areas of the skin are exposed to the radiation. Doctors supervise the therapy.

Based on the results of this study, health insurance companies in Germany were forced to accept and pay for climate therapy as an acceptable treatment for uveitis patients. This treatment is especially successful for patients whose illness may have endogenous and immunological causes.

Light therapy was further developed in cooperation with the

skin and eye clinic of the University of Münster. They proved that artificial light could be an alternative treatment for uveitis patients.

The confrontation with an acute or chronic phase of uveitis and its resulting problems, its unknown causes and uncertain prognosis, make for a dramatic situation for sufferers and their families. They often feel left alone with their illness, partially due to the fact that there is such a limited amount of information available on uveitis. Often their doctors can't help due to a lack of knowledge or time. That's why I initiated self-help groups. Since then about thirteen such groups meet regularly. Their purpose is to give mutual psychological support and to exchange new medical and scientific information among the participants.

My husband and I were rather surpised whe we heard about the success of our projects from Professor Busse, the director of the university eye clinic in Münster. He mentioned that the light and climate therapy we developed not only reduced the patients' suffering, but also reduced the cost of treatment by billions of marks. A rather nice success.

This was our incentive to initiate another preventive project within the field of eye medicine. In cooperation with Professor Busse and the university clinic of Münster, we want to administer preventive eye checkups in kindergartens in Münster and Gütersloh. Today children as young as six experience diminished eyesight. It is our goal to convince the Ministry of Health to include regular eye exams in the wellness program for children.

Let me mention that our youngest son's illness kept us on our toes until he was twenty-five years old. Phases of hope would alternate with phases of tears and desperation. Again and again he faced the danger of retinal detachment. But we were lucky, and he kept his eyesight. Today Andreas has completely recovered.

Manual Medicine

Prompted by personal experience, the Bertelsmann Foundation founded the Department of Alternative Medicine at the Westphalian Wilhelms University in Münster in 1993. When my husband was having back problems, we noticed that chiropractic therapy was relatively unknown in Germany, and that we had to travel as far as the Netherlands to find a chiropractor who could help him. The Academy of Manual Medicine in the Netherlands has existed for many years, and alternative medicine is an integral part of regular treatment plans in countries like the Netherlands, Switzerland, and the US. If you've ever been to America you know that there is a chiropractor on every street corner. In addition to a physician's training as an orthopedic specialist, it takes four additional years of study to become a chiropractor. These facts and my husband's personal experiences made us wonder whether Germany shouldn't have an academy of manual medicine as well. The answer was a resounding "yes."

The main reason for such an academy is that diseases of the movement apparatus and degenerative joint problems have become a national problem, because, if chronic, they ultimately may lead to the inability to work. Back and spine problems alone account for about 80 million sick days a year. The costs are alarming: in Germany one-third of about 33 billion German marks (US $17 billion) goes toward diagnosis, treatment, medication, physiotherapy, and the like, whereas the remaining two-thirds goes to the continuation of salaries during sick leave and disability, as well as the cost of a company's loss of productivity and the like. In addition, these diseases are also the main cause for early retirement.

Most university clinics and orthopedic departments focus their training, teaching, and research on surgical treatment methods, and so it is only natural that in the past, most orthopedic treatment plans used surgery. About 100,000 hip surgeries and about

80,000 knee surgeries are performed in Germany every year. And since about a third of the population will suffer from degenerative joint problems after the age of sixty, it can be expected that demographic changes will result in an increase of surgical procedures.

Yet only a small portion of the surgical treatments promises success. Only about 30 to 40 percent of back and spine problems can be treated successfully with traditional medicine. Therefore a growing number of patients no longer rely on medication, but turn to alternative natural treatment methods. Knowing all this inspired us to search for new treatment methods above and beyond traditional orthopedic medicine. In cooperation with the University of Münster, the Bertelsmann Foundation decided to support the training and education in, and research of, the treatment methods of alternative medicine in order to lead to an integration of traditional and alternative medicine.

Alternative medicine offers indispensable diagnostic methods by combining the knowldege and different methodologies from several disciplines, such as orthopedic medicine, rheumatology, neurology, and physics. Alternative medicine is largely based on experience rather than scientific proof, and we all know that researchers at universities are skeptical towards new and unproven methods. So the Academy founded by the Bertelsmann Foundation aims to raise the awareness and acceptance of alternative medicine by factually and competently defining its unique place within traditional medicine. The Academy supports development, research, and training of the therapeutic methods of alternative medicine.

The successful application of alternative medicine, as much as that of traditional medicine, depends more on the correct diagnosis than on treatment methods. Therefore alternative medicine uses an exact and detailed examination to diagnose joint and spine problems with the intention of finding the best possible treatment plan for the individual patient. Obviously, the success of the treatment also depends on the doctor's knowledge and skill. If an orthopedist is only trained in surgical orthopedic medicine, it is more likely that he will examine the patient with surgery in mind and will therefore suggest surgical intervention rather than other treatment options. We wanted to counteract this vicious circle by making alternative medicine part of traditional orthopedic medicine. Many orthopedic problems are caused by functional disturbances and can be treated with chiropractic methods and therapeutic exercises.

We founded an ambulatory treatment center where patients are treated with methods other than surgery to care for their orthopedic problems and taught to manage the pain that accompanies these problems. Alternative medicine uses techniques such as increased mobilization, manipulation, and neuromuscular treatments. In other words, alternative medicine comprises treatments of muscles and/or mobilization of the joints with neurophysiological mechanisms, behavioral training, movement therapies, and back exercises.

The Academy offers continuous patient care including orthopedic treatment, physiotherapy, and rehabilitation in cooperation with other institutions that may or may not be part of the university. The Academy focuses on the orthopedic therapy of children and adults, sports therapy, and interdisciplinary headache therapy.

It is muscle weakness that frequently causes back pain, and therefore specific training of the muscles to stabilize the spine may help manage back pain. A biomechanical analysis of the back muscles allows an exact diagnosis of the strengths and weaknesses of the particular muscle corsette. This "muscular profile" is the basis upon which the treatment and training plan of the individual patient is developed.

The Academy offers its patients a network of treatment methods including modern diagnosis with the technical assistance of X rays, ultrasounds, MRIs, or even three-dimensional video-optical measurements of the spine's surface. Optimal results and the patient's welfare are the ultimate goal of any and all collaboration among specialists from all areas of medicine within or outside the university.

In addition, the Academy offers education and training for physicians and physiotherapists in subjects such as pain management, alternative medicine, and chiropractic therapy. After successful participation the doctors earn the title Doctor of Chiropractic Medicine. The Academy also offers programs for students in subjects such as alternative diagnosis and therapy of the movement apparatus, lectures on pain management, and classes on clinical aspects of alternative therapy. Clinical research projects are also part of the Academy's program.

The express purpose of the Academy is to offer optimal conditions for all areas of therapy, education, training, and research in the field of alternative medicine. The combination of a high level of instruction with practice in state-of-the-art medical treatment methods is the ultimate goal.

The Next Health Project: Help with Metabolic Problems

At a meeting of retired employees, a woman told me she suffered from severe rheumatism. Even moving with a walker caused her great pain. But when I met her again nine months later, she didn't need the walker anymore and was free of pain. She was beaming. It seemed like a miracle. What was her secret? She told me that she had started taking high doses of vitamins, minerals, and micronutrients after she had read about this treatment in a magazine. After only a few weeks her condition had improved. I found this highly interesting. I asked myself if this was the idea for a new project, and whether researching this woman's experience was a good idea.

When, shortly after this encounter, my husband complained that his hand hurt when he wrote, I gave him a high dose of vitamins, minerals, and micronutrients. And surprise, surprise, it helped! A week later his pain was gone. This experience was the basis for a new project, in which we asked ourselves which diseases might be influenced by metabolic problems.

Many patients suffer from illnesses that today's medicine cannot successfully treat. Of course, our lifestyle, our working conditions, and other stress factors we deal with in modern times have led to the development of heretofore unknown illnesses. Not only the diseases of the elderly, but also those of children and infants seem to point the fact that some illnesses may have to do with problems of the metabolization of minerals, micronutrients, and vitamins.

These nutritional supplements have to be taken with the right amount of food in order for the body to absorb them properly. A lack of any or all of them may have negative consequences, whereby deficiencies manifest themselves differently in each patient. Usually patents suffer from rather unspecific symptoms. Pressure situations such as stress, intensive exercise, pregnancy and breastfeeding, heavy consumption of alcohol and tobacco, extreme diets, a lack of exercise, junk food, or even intestinal problems caused by old age may lead to a deficiency of minerals, micronutrients, and vitamins, which in turn may lead to serious health problems.

We initiated a blood screening among 298 employees of the Bertelsmann Foundation and Bertelsmann AG to test the amounts of minerals, micronutrients and vitamins in their blood.

We were very surprised to find that almost all participants showed a deficiency of one or more of the following:

Magnesium 41%
Zinc 40%
Selenium 50%
Vitamin B$_{12}$ 46%
Vitamin E 12%

This was even more surprising considering that most participants in the study were rather young.

There are still physicians in Germany who maintain that if a person eats healthily and regularly, he or she will not suffer from a deficiency of vitamins, minerals, and micronutrients. However, all the participants in our study had been convinced that they were eating healthily, and they were rather surprised when they received results that proved otherwise. The discrepancies between the micronutrients we discovered in the blood of our participants and the apparently healthy diet they were following were rather remarkable. We assume that there could have been various reasons for this.

First of all, many families obviously don't really know enough about shopping for, combining, and preparing the right foods correctly so that the nutrients stay intact. If you store or prepare food incorrectly, the food loses the nutrients. The food served in the company cafeterias of about 15 million workers and employees across Germany does not contain the necessary amount of micronutrients. And nutritional deficiency may also be caused by eating habits formed by long working hours which favor fast food over home-cooked meals.

We also realized that eating too much may result in a deficiency of vitamins or other nutrients. Children, older people, pregnant women and breastfeeding mothers, people engaging in professional sports, smokers, alcoholics, and those with one-sided diets such as vegetarians are at a high risk to suffer from a deficiency of nutrients. The same is true for people with intestinal or liver problems.

The effects of a vitamin deficiency may range from fatigue, to reduced physical and intellectual abilities, to frequent infections, mood swings, and even to growth problems in children. It is important to consider that only a serious and long-lasting deficiency results in noticeable problems, and that such a deficiency is very rarely concentrated on just one specific substance.

Self-medication, i.e., taking supplements without a doctor's advice or prescription, is rather common. Germans consume millions of pills and capsules every single year. This is because people want to take care of themselves, of course, but without realizing it they may actually be exposing themselves to a great danger. You have to imagine that vitamins, minerals, and micronutrients work together like the instruments of an orchestra. If one instrument is missing, or plays too loudly or too softly, the harmony is disturbed. It is no different with nutrients: If we have too many or too little, the metabolism comes apart at the seams and disorders may develop. The effect of one micronutrient in the body always needs to be seen in the context of other nutritional elements. Too much or too little of one micronutrient may have negative implications on the effect of one or more other micronutrients.

But who really knows how they work together and affect each other? Of course we know today that a lack of fluoride leads to tooth decay, but what is the effect of too much or too little vitamin C? Many people don't really think about their health, or the symptoms and/or effects of vitamin deficiency.

Since a blood screening can show a vitamin deficiency before it has implications to your health, I suggest that everyone take such a blood test before resorting to self-medication. Unfortunately, health insurance doesn't always pay for such a blood test. Be that as it may, you should consult a physician before you medicate yourself with supplements for any extended period of time.

The Bertelsmann Foundation has created informational guidelines for medical practitioners regarding the clinical aspects and chemical analysis of vitamins, minerals, and micronutrients. We also created guidelines for the consumer to contribute to education and awareness among the population.

I take the blood test annually, and then diligently take what micronutrients my doctor recommends, such as vitamin C, vitamin E, and magnesium, which are very important. Magnesium, a protective micronutrient, averts heart palpitations by relaxing the muscles, widening the blood vessels, and improving the circulatory system in general.

My experience has shown me that, unless they suffer from hereditary diseases, everyone can be the manager of his or her own health.

My Suggestions for a Healthy Lifestyle

I believe that you can learn to deal with stress. I am more productive and can handle more stress today than I could when I was young. Many health crises have taught me to listen to my body and to find out what is good for me and what I need to be productive. Like so many occasions before, I followed my husband's example. His credo has always been, "A healthy mind in a healthy body." He bicycles ten or more miles every day and goes hiking on a regular basis. On vacations he goes swimming and hiking in the mountains. Even at eighty years of age he is a very flexible and active person. He eats with moderation, drinks very little alcohol, and doesn't smoke. This helps him to remain slender, and he doesn't carry a big belly in front of him like so many other men his age. Just imagine: Ten pounds too many means that you are carrying forty sticks of butter around with you. What a burden.

I have learned from my husband that you cannot take your health for granted. You have to do something for it, and work at it with discipline.

Not a single day goes by without exercise, and I even get up ninety minutes early so I can do my morning fitness routine: I begin with a three- to four-mile run, then I go on a fifteen- to twenty-minute swim, and finally I do back exercises. I follow this routine diligently in any weather, so I'd really miss something if I had to go a day without it. I've noticed that my metabolism and my circulation function better since I've started on this routine. I feel better mentally as well, because exercise can relax stress and counteract aggression. Movement frees endorphins in your body, the "good-mood" hormones, if you will. Since I've started this routine, I've been much more balanced and in better spirits in general. In addition, I've quit smoking—I used to smoke thirty or more cigarettes a day. I've been following a healthy diet for the past five years, and I drink more than a gallon of water or tea (I prefer a mixture of chamomile and peppermint) every day. I've lost about ten pounds (I wear a size 4), and feel much healthier and more productive than when I was younger.

Sometimes I spend up to six hours a day, five days a week in conferences. I have noticed that many people have trouble concentrating for that long. I have no problem with that. I think what helps is on those days I eat very little and drink a lot—about a gallon of water or my special mixture of health tea—in order to not burden my body with digestion, which would draw the blood from my head to the center of my body and make me tired. I stay awake and alert. And in the evening I can enjoy a full, yet light, meal—I prefer fish and vegetables.

Caring solely for the body, however, is not the point. Such a lifestyle would be false, because soul and body are united, and it is necessary to avoid one-sidedness. Physical as well as psychological and intellectual fitness makes you feel good and self-confident.

And there's something else that helps me cope with the daily grind: positive thinking. It's a wonderful well of strength that helps me to remain mentally healthy. My optimistic attitude helps a great deal. I have a joyful and merry disposition, and I'm not depressed and grouchy. Obviously this is a genetic inheritance from my mother, who had a very similar disposition. I've consciously developed this positive attitude.

Positive thinking has taught me that I create my experiences myself. I know how powerful negative thoughts can be, and so I have learned to control my thinking based on the motto, "You are what you think." Thinking is conscious, which essentially means that you can control your experiences by choosing your thoughts, beliefs, and emotions. The Greek philosopher Epictetus said, "We are not moved by the things, but by the opinions we have about these things." With regard to success in life, our only problem is ourselves. It is not other people or our circumstances that create difficulties, it is rather the manner in which we approach other people and our attitude toward these circumstances. A change of attitude will bring about a change of situation. A positive attitude can influence you and the way you communicate with others. Our lives are in our own hands!

I have worked hard on my attitude toward people and situations. Every single day I consciously list the things I am thankful for in order to see the positive things in life more clearly. This helps me feel joy and fight my worries. I tell myself: I am, I can, I will! This motivates me, and even difficult situations can be mastered. On many occasions I've felt that such an attitude makes life easier and more beautiful. Every day I am grateful that I am healthy and creative, and that I can shape my own life.

We constantly hear about hazards to our health. I think that every single human being is responsible for his or her health. The German healthcare system works according to the principle of solidarity, and I find it to be against the very spirit of solidarity if you neglect your health. If the costs of healthcare rise, all members have to pay. If every insured person were to develop an awareness of health issues, fewer people would need medical treatment, and the costs would go down. Many people have no awareness of their body and take their health for granted. This attitude will not keep you fit into old age. If you don't honor your body, you don't honor your soul. Such an attitude can cause psychosomatic illnesses.

You need to love yourself in order to love others. Is this the key to the growing lack of love in our world? In our drive for success, money, and status, do we forget not only others, but ourselves as well?

A healthy lifestyle prevents illness. Weight control and a sensible diet can be the first step to avoid illness. Even traditional medicine acknowledges this, because a number of chronic diseases cannot be treated adequately with traditional treatments. Chinese medicine, for example, has always maintained the importance of preventive measures. In ancient China, the physician was only paid when the patient was healthy; when the patient fell ill, he stopped paying.

Preventive medicine maintains the importance of a healthy diet. Following just a few pieces of advice might improve your health: eat whole-grain breads rather than white, drink orange juice or milk rather than soda or lemonade. I prefer to serve fresh fruit and raw vegetables, carefully prepared vegetables, low-fat dairy products, and fish or small portions of lean meat. I find it particularly important to make sure that I eat a balanced meal after a stressful day in order to replenish my body with the right amount of minerals, micronutrients, and vitamins. My goal is to minimize the risks that come with a lack of concentration, with fatigue, sleeplessness, anxiety, and a loss of productivity. It is also important to avoid the overconsumption of alcohol. When I travel I take especially good care of my health to counteract the effects of a nutrition my body may not be used to, as well as of jet lag and climate changes. For the love of our health and our children we should observe a few basic rules of nutrition.

Children and Nutrition

It is especially important to make sure children follow a healthy diet. It is important to watch the ingredients of their breakfast and their snacks at school. White rolls with jelly or Nutella[1], candy, lemonade or soda with sugar not only offer very little roughage, but very few nutrients.

I think it is wrong and careless of so many parents to send their children to school without breakfast. And the habit of giving the children money so they can buy something for themselves during the day is not very smart either, because the money usually goes towards candy or sweetened soft drinks. Such a diet won't help children concentrate and compete. Hidden fats in cold cuts on

[1] A popular European chocolate-hazelnut spread.

sandwiches are not healthy either, and may contribute to weight problems. Allowing such a diet is reckless endangerment of our children's health at a stage when they are still growing and developing. It is much better to create the fun snacks suggested in so many women's magazines.

Due to their biorhythms and the demands at school, children and teenagers need more than a third of their entire day's energy in the morning. Therefore a breakfast that doesn't supply the necessary amount of vitamins, minerals, and micronutrients may lead to physiological imbalances which may lead to agression or apathy, and a diminished attention span or reaction time, which in turn may lead to accidents. Growth problems that may not be noticeable until much later (such as osteoporosis) may occur if there is a deficiency of micronutrients while children are still growing and maturing. Iron, calcium, and folic acid are especially important for children and teenagers.

Diseases caused by nutritional deficiencies account for about 100 million German marks (US $50 million) of health-related costs.

We are in the process of establishing guidelines for an intensive educational program on nutrition and eating habits. The interdisciplinary round of experts called for my Committee on Nutrition and Health brings together nutritionists, dermatologists, geriatric specialists, and specialists in children's nutrition. In cooperation with the Academy for Nutritional Medicine in Hannover, we want to collect expert knowledge and start a discussion on the relevance of nutrition to health issues. Our ultimate goal is to raise public awareness.

Our first target is school-age children. We want them to be aware of their specific nutritional situation and improve their nutrition and develop healthy eating habits. Allergies and posture problems have increased dramatically, afflictions that may be caused by nutrition (too sweet and too fatty) and a lack of exercise. Elementary school kids exercise less than one hour a day. Many children do not have access to playgrounds or gyms or just plain nature where they could test and increase their dexterity, strength, and endurance. Some children cannot even climb anymore or walk backward, because they have become too stiff. Every other child suffers from muscle weakness, every fifth child complains about back pain, and every sixth child between six and eight years is overweight. Nationwide school examinations have revealed that the number of overweight children in Germany has risen to more than two million.

Eating habits are established in childhood and youth, and it is very difficult to change them as an adult. Considering that good nutrition may assist in the prevention of illnesses, I believe that children and teenagers should learn about it at school. Members of the medical profession have demanded that the subject of health education be mandatory in schools, particularly as a means of fighting alcohol and nicotine abuse. The president of the Federal Medical Board, Jörg Dietrich Hoppe, says, "Apart from home, school is the only place where young people can learn about the dangers of unhealthy habits."

According to a study of the World Health Organization, among 120,000 children from 28 nations, 8 percent of eleven-year-old boys, and 4 percent of eleven-year-old girls take tranquilizers at least once a month. I find that alarming!

The major common diseases strongly influenced by nutritional factors are cancer, stroke, diabetes, heart-lung diseases, weight problems, and intestinal disorders that influence the immune system. It is assumed that with better nutrition about 30 to 40 percent of cancers could be avoided. Estimates claim that problems caused by unhealthy diets account for about 100 billion German marks (US $50 billion) of health-related costs each year. Some of these costs could be saved if the population were to change eating habits. This is why the roundtable Nutrition and Popular Diseases deals with the relationship of nutrition to individual diseases. Which nutritional factors may help avoid the development of a particular disease, and which may help it along? What would an optimal nutritional program look like to prevent diseases?

What diet should be followed once an illness has struck? How does nutrition influence the course of the disease? We want to create informational materials and make nutritional suggestions to the consumer as well as to physicians, nutritionists, diet consultants, and teachers.

In addition, a round of experts is working on the relationship between nutrition and the development of breast cancer. This question has haunted me ever since I learned, on a visit to Japan, that Japanese women suffer from breast cancer less frequently than European women. Experts believe that this is due to nutritional factors, because the Japanese eat many more soy products and much more fish than Europeans, and Japanese women living in America suffer from breast cancer as much as Americans of other ethnic backgrounds. There are clear research results that support the idea that nutrition plays a major role in the development of breast cancer. Therefore we hope to be able to come up wtih preventive nutritional measures to avoid this devastating illness.

Professor Peter Brätter, one of our research consultants who has developed numerous guidelines for physicians and consumers, points out that antioxidants such as carotenes and vitamin C protect the cells from so-called free radicals, aggressive oxygen groups that harm the cells. An analysis of secondary plant substances and their influence on the development and growth of tumors has given serious indications that beta-carotene and phytoestrogens (estrogen from plants) may diminish the risk of breast cancer.

Scientists, however, want proof rather than anecdotes. Therefore we are still faced with more questions than answers. Of course, other risk factors for breast cancer are a lack of exercise, alcohol consumption, and genetics. Whether the consumption of soy or wheat products can actually deter the development of breast cancer has not been scientifically proven. It cannot be denied, however, that a healthy diet of five vegetable meals a day, with little fat and little alcohol, is very sensible. Therefore, until there is proof for a relationship between nutrition and cancer, experts suggest that everyone follow these simple nutritional guidelines.

We hope that the nutritional commission of the Bertelsmann Foundation scheduled for next year can present more findings to the population.

10. The German Stroke Foundation

I started the German Stroke Foundation in 1992, based in part on a personal experience.

At the age of fourteen one of my sons began to feel some numbness in his left foot, which then moved up the entire left leg. We went from physician to physician, but nobody seemed able to determine the cause of this sensation. During a vacation in Spain I noticed that my son, for no apparent reason, frequently fell down, and I really began to worry (although I tried not to show it). Upon returning from our vacation, we again went from doctor to doctor, all of whom told me that, neurologically, he was fine and that his troubles could be related to developmental problems. They didn't seem to think it was anything serious, but I was terribly worried. Four days after our most recent doctor visit, I received a call from my son at the office. "Mom," he said, "I can't walk anymore." Any mother or father can imagine the shock and disbelief I felt. I dropped everything immediately, rushed home, picked him up and took him to the hospital in Hannover. I will never forget this trip. I held him in my arms tightly, trying to comfort him. My hands were shaking and my thoughts were racing, trying to fight my own sense of desperation. What did fate have in store for us?

Once again I found myself waiting in the barren hallways of a hospital while my son was being examined. As nurses ran about busily, I just sat there, watching them, as if paralyzed by the worry, fear, and helplessness I felt. What was going on with my child?

The doctors didn't have an answer. My son was paralyzed on his left side, and the fear was that his heart and lungs might be affected as well. That would have ended his life. But after two long and fearful days we knew that our son would live. But we didn't yet know, though, what his life would look like, or whether he would need constant care.

Fortunately, his paralysis was only temporary, and six weeks later my son could walk again. The whole incident was a mystery to the neurologists—they just couldn't figure out what had happened. All they knew was that it wasn't a stroke. The most reasonable assumption they eventually came up with was that a tick had been responsible, because our son had been playing a lot with our German shepherds in the park. To this day we have not been able to completely solve this mystery.

As difficult as this situation was for our family, something positive finally came of it, because this incident set the course for the German Stroke Foundation, which has been able to help a great number of people. The neurologists I met during my son's illness had asked me for help with a research project on the early detection of stroke. At the time, the diagnosis and treatment of stroke were far more difficult than they are today. Usually the only available treatment option was the surgical removal of the blood clot. After careful consideration, I decided to steer the Bertelsmann Foundation into a project on the diagnosis and prevention of brain disorders in cooperation with the university clinics of Düsseldorf and Münster. Upon completion of this project, which involved the continued development and testing of detection technology called Doppler sonography, the experts approached me again, this time complaining that stroke victims were entirely without any government lobby. At the time, a very well-known heart surgeon told me, "As far as patients go, stroke victims are the poorest of the poor." Their disabilities are clearly visible and require a high amount of extremely specialized care. You cannot comprehend the amount of suffering the victims and their families have to go through unless you've had firsthand experience with the affliction.

The physicians who approached me informed me of the effects of this insidious and widespread disorder: Stroke is the third most common cause of death in Germany, with anywhere from 250,000 to 300,000 people suffering from stroke each year. There may be even more cases, since not every stroke is diagnosed as such. Every fifth victim will die, more than half of the victims will suffer lifelong disability, and only a quarter of the victims will eventually be able to return to work. After a stroke, about 17 percent of the victims recover partially, and only 6 percent recover completely. The economic costs are estimated at about 10 to 15 billion German marks (US $5 to $10 billion) every year, due in part to the fact that a stroke is the most common cause for loss of employment.

One of the major challenges for the medical community is the early detection and diagnosis of stroke. To physicians it seemed extremely important to find preventive measures, including the awareness and education of physicians and the population, as well as improved treatment methods that would increase the survival rate of stroke victims. It was apparent that stroke victims were in desperate need of help and support.

The physicians I had been working with thus far suggested I head a new foundation to deal with the issues surrounding strokes. When I told my husband about this idea his response was, "If you want to do this, you are on your own. I cannot help you build a foundation, because I am too busy to take on new responsibilities at the moment."

I asked for time to think. I knew nothing of the subject, and I didn't even know anyone among my family or friends who had suffered a stroke. When people think of a stroke, they think of old age, disabilties, complete personality loss, infirmity, and ultimately death. I had my doubts that I'd be able to make the general population care about this insidious disease, because most people want to enjoy only the beautiful and pleasant things of life while denying such terrible blows of fate. The subject of stroke brings about associations of a life with a distorted mouth, speech impediments, and other physical disabilities for which our fast-paced society has no room. And many people believe that only old people can suffer a stroke.

Yet the more I learned about the subject, the more I felt that these people really did need my help. I began to come to a decision: I wanted to do whatever I could to improve the situation of stroke victims. Before I began my work, I tried to get as much information about the disease as I could. I visited intensive care units in hospitals and rehabilitation centers where stroke victims were cared for, I watched brain surgeries, and I talked with victims. Some of them were as helpless as infants.

It soon became apparent to me that neither physicians nor the general population knew enough about strokes and their implications, risks, and warning signs. Many people think that such a fate will only befall others, yet the reality is very different, and the number of victims is increasing. One-third of our population is sixty and older. Due to the development of the age pyramid (more and more older people, fewer and fewer younger people) the number of stroke victims will rise even more. And more and more young people are among the victims, a fact that neither the general population nor, unfortunately, the medical community, seems to realize. I wanted to counteract this, and I sensed immediately that this was a worthwhile undertaking. I wanted to take action and initiate things. Considering how many people I could potentially help with this foundation, I sensed that I was needed. It was a great challenge.

The Beginning

I had raised about 700,000 German marks (US $350,000) with the last Rose Ball benefit, and I decided that this would be my starting capital. The foundation began with but a small team consisting of one general manager, an assistant, and me.

At first we had many lively discussions with physicians in an attempt to find a different name for this disease, because I found the term "stroke" disturbing. In the end we weren't able to find a better term, and today I am happy about the fact that neither the word "stroke" nor its associations are taboo. Today it is possible to say, "I had a stroke, but I am able to lead a worthwhile life." This means that we were able to meet one of the foundation's goals.

The improvement of treatment during and after an acute stroke was another goal of the foundation. Many hospitals and physicians' offices aren't able to diagnose a stroke quickly and accurately enough to treat the victims adequately. We wanted to support the continuing education and training of physicians and the hospital and ambulance staff. After all, the latter are usually the first with the victim.

In addition to raising public and physicians' awareness, we wanted to create a national network of stroke stations with the necessary medical equipment for quick and adequate treatment which would save lives and decrease the lasting effects of stroke. While it is possible to treat and reverse the damage done after a heart attack for up to twelve hours, a stroke only allows a window of about four to six hours to reverse any effects. Once this window closes, chances are the victim will suffer lifelong paralysis, speech, or vision impairments. Unknowingly, many family physicians used to wait until the next day to treat a stroke victim, and ambulance personnel often wouldn't even turn on the siren when rushing a stroke victim to the hospital. Failing to administer correct treatment quickly results in irreversible damages. We wanted to avoid this.

Prevention is better than treatment. This is always true, and especially so for a stroke. Even though tremendous progress has been made with regard to the treatment and rehabilitation of stroke victims, the chances for complete recovery are still relatively small. The damage is often irreversible and so severe that only long and arduous therapy may enable the victim to live a barely normal life despite his affliction. But now there is hope. The great strides made in brain research and treatment in the last five years promise unimagined medical possibilities.

Nonetheless, prevention is necessary. Experts claim that about 70 percent of all strokes could be avoided by something as simple as the awareness of one's own genetic predisposition, which affects about a third of all stroke victims. An attempt to decrease other risk factors, such as high blood pressure, heart disease, arteriosclerosis, diabetes, smoking, and a lack of exercise is important in the fight against stroke as well.

This is the situation we faced at the outset of our endeavor. Therefore, our first and foremost goal was to raise awareness among the general population, in hospitals, and among practicing physicians. We brought together an alliance of physicians, economists, media specialists, and citizens, all of us working toward the same goal. Professor Meffert of the University of Münster donated the entire marketing concept, and the individual campaigns were donated by the advertising agency of Springer & Jacobi, Hamburg. And I especially want to mention the support of the pharmaceutical industry in Germany.

All of these committed parties volunteered their services. Their priceless generosity has given me so much strength and courage.

Making Contacts and Raising Money

It was the beginning of a very tough and exhausting period for me, during which I had to get up between four and five in the morning in order to meet early with sponsors and project partners. I'd been able to raise about 31 million German marks (US $16 million) for the new Foundation so far. The name Mohn and my connection to the Bertelsmann media empire might have helped quite a bit, but in the end, whether or not a meeting with a sponsor is successful depends on my ability to make my point to the prospective sponsor. It's the personal level that counts.

I usually start off these dialogues with questions about today's concepts of company management and leadership of its personnel, because these are topics that interest everyone in business. Of course I need to be well informed about the person I am meeting and the company he or she works for. So I need to read company reports and get mentally prepared for the meeting. It is only after I've successfully created an atmosphere of trust that I mention my actual request—the German Stroke Foundation.

In most cases thus far I've been successful. Once I've managed to open the potential sponsors' hearts for stroke victims, once I've managed to make them understand that support is needed, we can all work together. In my meetings I try to explain the implications of a stroke for the victims and their families. We all have our dreams . . . a beautiful condo or a house, travel, professional success, good health as we grow old with our spouses. Whatever the dream, a stroke turns it into an instant nightmare. It is a nightmare haunting 250,000 Germans year after year, a nightmare in which, in the blink of an eye, one's life falls apart.

At first I had many meetings with entrepreneurs. I remember one incident in particular, a meeting with Helmuth Maucher who, at the time, was chairman of the board of Nestlé. I'd first met him at a conference on the Petersberg in Bonn twenty years ago. He knew that I was dealing with medical research, and so he invited me to come visit the Nestlé headquarters in Vevey, Switzerland, to see their nutritional research center. This meeting started off in an embarrassing manner for me, because my flight had been delayed, and, since we had arranged to meet in a hotel restaurant, I was unable to reach him to inform him of my delay. When I finally reached his wife, she told me that he had already left for our meeting, and so, over an hour later, I found Mr. Maucher waiting patiently in the hotel lobby. His greeting was still very warm and friendly, and he answered my apologies with a charming smile. "Don't worry about your delay, Mrs. Mohn," he said, "this way I had an entire hour to look forward to our reunion." He is a real gentleman.

We discussed many interesting subjects on that evening. In a thank-you note I later wrote, I asked him for support for my foundation. His answer was prompt. Nestlé was going to finance an international workshop on "The Relationship Between Nutrition and Stroke" and other projects. This company contact has proven to be very valuable to this day.

Not every meeting is that easy and harmonious. Sometimes

the conversations take a lot of effort and strength on my part. Once, in a meeting with a middle-class entrepreneur, my colleague and I were met with a rather frosty atmosphere. The man wouldn't let on whether I'd been able to inspire him into supporting the fight against stroke. I was very insecure when we left, particularly because the good-byes had been very cold. But once we were on the street I remembered my mother's credo, "Don't ever give up," and my usual optimism returned. No, this meeting was not going to stop me; I was going to continue to fight for my stroke victims. "Tomorrow is another day," I said to my colleague, and off we went for a cup of coffee. I ended up getting a rather large contribution from this entrepreneur anyway.

My work for the the German Stroke Foundation created many new connections that proved valuable to our company as well. One of these contacts was Dr. Jürgen Strube, chairman of the board of BASF AG. I initially met with him to request financial support, but the actual topic at the lunch we shared at the BASF guest house in Ludwigshafen was the implications globalization had for companies and the media. I found Dr. Strube to have a very strong personality with tremendous leadership qualities, a person we'd like to have at Bertelsmann. He was a goal-oriented man of great character, yet honest and modest. Back in Gütersloh I told my husband about Dr. Strube, and together we discussed how we might engage him in our work at Bertelsmann. At first he became a member of the advisory council of the Bertelsmann Foundation, and to this day we welcome having his ideas and skills at our disposal. Soon he will become a member of the Board, and at the same time part of the Bertelsmann Property Management Division.

In addition to the support from companies and businesses, we also find support from committed individuals with a good heart. I was so touched by the efforts of the *Landfrauenverbandes Lette* in the Münster Valley, a women's group known for collecting and selling recipes of the region in popular cookbooks. They approached me with a request to speak before them, and I was so taken by this idea that we arranged it immediately. And what did

I find waiting there for me but coffee, cake, liquor, women of all ages, and a check for more than 50,000 German marks (US $25,000), raised entirely from the sale of their cookbooks. These people were obviously living according to a true sense of solidarity and compassion. I felt good among them and stayed much longer than I had time for. It was a really nice afternoon. It has given me something to remember forever.

Like these generous women, many other people have helped me, and I am very grateful to them all. One of the greatest hurdles to overcome at first were the divergent needs and interests of the experts from various disciplines. It seemed so difficult to get all of them, particularly the neurologists, to sit down at one table. Often I found myself wondering whether the participants were truly interested in helping stroke victims, or if perhaps their own research projects were more important. It was disappointing to realize that some of them did have ulterior motives. It seemed like the Foundation was headed for a crisis, and I wondered night and day whether I'd have to give up. All I had wanted was the best, and I had devoted everything to the cause . . . my strength, my idealism, my patience, and my time. I couldn't help but be devastated by the fact that my efforts and commitment seemed to be in vain. I was worried and full of doubt. So one morning, over coffee, I poured out my heart to my husband. "I don't think I can do it," I said, "I'm at the end of my rope. I may have to give up." My husband knew how important the work, the Foundation, and the stroke victims really were to me. He understood my desperation and my worries. So he asked, "Will you continue your work if I take on the leadership of the Foundation?"

I didn't have to think about that very long. Of course I'd continue. Once again my husband had come to my rescue and given me new courage, strength, and optimism. His offer of support was particularly meaningful to me since he had declined to get involved at the outset. He became vice chairman of the board and, with his great management experience and people skills, he was able to create order out of the chaos of individual interests. Suddenly the future of the foundation was much brighter.

Raising Awareness

The most important aspect of our work was to educate the general population, because according to research, only about 7 percent would even recognize the first signs of a stroke. At the same time we wanted to intensify the continuing education of general practicioners, hospital employees, and ambulance staff, because if the ambulance staff is able to quickly administer proper first-aid treatment, lives may be saved.

In 1996 we started our first awareness campaign. We distributed ten million questionnaires in pharmacies, magazines and ICE[2] trains. Two hundred thousand people filled them out and returned them, mostly people with high risk factors such as high blood pressure and other blood disorders, diabetes, or obesity. The results of the questionnaire were therefore not representative, and we couldn't draw any general conclusions. But the campaign was very meaningful with regard to the preventive medical measures needed for persons at risk. All in all, up through the year 2000, we've reached about one hundred million people with this print, TV, and radio campaign.

The Foundation's Infomobile started traveling through Germany in 1997. The van is much more than information on wheels, for it also offers a medical examination and advice to the population. The van is equipped with state-of-the-art computers and medical equipment, and is staffed by a team of two, a physician and a driver. Their stops are announced in the local media.

The main focus of the Infomobile is a ten-minute test assessing an individual's risk factor by creating an individual stroke profile. The most important factors are the individual's blood pressure and cholesterol level. They are measured in the Infomobile, and the physician on board interprets them in light of the individual's medical history. The Infomobile serves about fifty to sixty people a day.

[2] ICE trains are inter-city rapid transit trains.

The results the Infomobile has gathered so far are rather interesting. Seven percent of the participants fall under a high risk category, 27 percent are in a low to medium risk group, and 66 percent of the population show very low to no risk. These numbers are based on the 14,800 participants examined by the Infomobile so far.

Due to the great demand for these examinations, the Infomobile is booked months in advance. So we needed a second Infomobile, and fortunately we've managed to get one quickly and easily. During a trip I approached Dr. Mangold, a board member of DaimlerChrysler. "Dr. Mangold," I said, "we need a second Infomobile." His response was simple: "You'll get it from us, Mrs. Mohn." I am so happy whenever things get done on a personal level. It's so uncomplicated, because you're met with personal help and understanding.

The first symptoms of a stroke are often so minimal that many people don't recognize them as such. But at least a third of all strokes have announced themselves before. These early symptoms are precisely the ones the victim will exhibit during an acute stroke: temporary blindness or vision disturbances in one eye, double vision, one-sided paralysis or numbness in the arms or legs, speech impediments, dizziness, and a sudden splitting headache. If any of these symptoms occur, it is paramount to consult a physician, whether they disappear after a few moments or not.

More and more young people are having strokes. Just a short while ago I visited a twenty-four-year-old woman with one-sided paralysis in the hospital. What's alarming is that her case is not rare. Our lifestyle is responsible for the increase of stroke among young people. Strokes are often brought on by one's lifestyle. The list of bad habits is long: time pressures, stress, lack of exercise, obesity, poor nutrition, smoking even while on the Pill, and a lot of coffee—this is the lifestyle many young men and women have chosen these days.

According to a widely respected research study, preventive

measures could avoid many strokes. Successful prevention requires the recognition of at-risk individuals, who can then diminish their risk through guided treatment or a specific change in habits.

One of the preventive measures is the lowering of blood pressure through healthier nutrition: little salt, little fat (if any), and plant fats instead of animal fats. Alcohol in moderation is not only permitted, but actually recommended . . . a glass of wine or beer each day is healthy. More, however, is hazardous to your health.

You shouldn't smoke at all. If you stop smoking, your risk factors drop by about 30 percent after one year, and after four to five years they drop to that of a nonsmoker. It is very beneficial to stop smoking, considering the tragic effects a stroke has on its victims and their families.

Tragic Fates

In literally a single stroke, life changes from one moment to the next for stroke victims and their families in unimaginable ways. A self-confident person in full command of his or her life and success suddenly becomes a helpless victim in need of constant care. It is an immeasurable tragedy for everyone affected.

While visiting a rehab center in Berlin, I met a forty-four-year-old man who had been a successful manager, happily living his carefree life with his wife and two children (five and eight years old) until the stroke hit. He was completely paralyzed, except for his eyelids, which now are his only means of communication. His brain is affected so badly that he is crying constantly. He was just lying there, helpless, covered in sweat, in need of twenty-four-hour nursing care, and without any hope for recovery.

The worst of it was that his family couldn't afford to pay for his stay at the clinic indefinitely, and so he was released to his family, who will care for him at home for the rest of his life. The physical and emotional stress his wife and children will have to bear night and day is hard to imagine.

I couldn't sleep that night. The image of this helpless man and thoughts of his family kept me awake. In these hours I realize how important and meaningful my work is for many people. Eighty percent of stroke victims are being cared for at home by their spouses and other family members.

These encounters make me very pensive. In light of these tragedies my own worries suddenly seem so small and petty. I am grateful that I can walk and exercise, that I can clearly see the beauty of the world, that I can laugh and cry . . . in short, I am grateful that I can live a normal life. In such moments I realize what a gift a healthy body and a healthy mind is, and I vow to never take that for granted, like most of us do much of the time.

Friends often ask me how I can handle constantly being around sick people and their sad stories. They would get depressed. Do I get depressed? No. I must have a lot of strength, because it is precisely these encounters that actually motivate me to continue my work. My positive hands-on nature helps a great deal. If someone needs assistance I don't complain, but immediately think about what I can do to help. I look for solutions and don't take time for discouraging thoughts.

"Do good deeds, and they will come back to you." This phrase comes true for me every single day. A grateful look from the eyes of a victim, a handshake, a nice letter . . . these things show me how much I am needed. It makes me feel that my life has some meaning.

Just a short while ago someone called me at our vacation home on Mallorca to ask for advice regarding an acquaintance who had suffered a stroke. The caller was so happy to have finally reached me. "I was looking for you," he said. I was able to help by recommending physicians and hospitals that might be helpful in this particular situation.

After the call I went outside on our terrace and looked out over the ocean. A feeling of insightful melancholy overwhelmed me. Thinking about the victim, I sent all my good thoughts for recovery his way, hoping that he would receive the appropriate therapy based on the information I had just passed on. Suddenly the sky seemed bluer, the sun brighter, the mountains more majestic than ever before. The chirping of crickets, the splendid array of colors and the scent of flowers . . . my senses were alert and ready to take in the beauty of nature with an intensity I had never before felt. Gratitude for my life, my health, my family, and for the opportunities fate had given me filled my heart. It was but a brief moment, happy and painful at the same time, yet I felt honored to have been able to experience it at all, and at such a beautiful place.

Is it possible that those in need give those who help them something in return? Maybe they heighten our awareness and sharpen our view for what's important. "Do good deeds, and they will come back to you." Indeed this has been my experience over and over again.

I was very touched by the book *My Year Off* by Robert McCrum, editor of a British publishing house, who had suffered a stroke at forty-one. Lying on his bedroom floor, fully conscious, aware that his body would no longer respond, that he was paralyzed on his left side, he waited for an endless hour for help to arrive and rush him to the hospital.

He decribes how he felt ripped away from his daily life, cut off from his old carefree, fun, and successful life. Now he feared for the future. It was hard to understand him when he spoke, and he felt like an infant. He was desperate during his time "off." He had spent his entire life cultivating his independence, only to find himself completely dependent, immobile, and passive. He was irritable, depressed, and easily annoyed. He felt helpless, stupid, vulnerable, and embarrassed, caught between "the spirit of a young man and the body of an old man." The healing process was long and arduous. ". . . On the rare days that my left side began to respond, it was as though I had discovered a sixth dimension. Such moments of joy were rare; I cried a lot in the hospital.

Sometimes the tears were slow and weepy; at others, uncontrolled and desperate. I could cry for any reason and none; I was told that this is characteristic of stroke victims."

"Writing the book has been a way to make sense of an extraordinary personal upheaval," writes McCrum. "It's also intended to show those of us who are well what it can be like when our bodies let us down in the midst of the lives we take for granted." And the book is intended to give hope, to show that recovery after a stroke is indeed possible.

Results So Far

After only seven years the German Stroke Foundation shows impressive results. We have established nearly one hundred stroke stations, where teams of neurologists and X-ray specialists are ready to help stroke victims as quickly and skillfully as possible. Their essential equipment includes ultrasound diagnostic machines, computer tomography, and machinery for cardiological examinations. Establishing one such center costs between 500,000 and 1.3 million German marks (between US $250,000 and $650,000), and experts claim that about 200 more are needed nationwide. A bed in a stroke station costs about 1,000 German marks (US $500) a day, and every station has four to six intensive care beds. In short, there is still a lot of work ahead of us.

A stroke center is important to a stroke victim's recovery. Clinical and technical supervision, intensive care, as well as early rehabilitation and speech therapy aim at avoiding later lifelong disabilities and complicated side effects.

The success of these stations is already visible. The death rate caused by strokes in the vicinity of such centers has dropped by 28 percent, and stroke victims suffer from considerably fewer permanent disablities. In addition, the stroke centers have reduced the typical hospital stay from three weeks to two. In general, the instant care given at the stroke centers has reduced the cost of treatment by about 40 percent.

Due to the Foundation's educational work, victims reach the hospital much sooner, because of an awareness of how important it is to receive help quickly. Physicians can only help adequately if they can help quickly.

One hundred and forty representatives of the medical community volunteer for us regionally, teaching seminars for victims and their families, and conducting continuing education programs for practicing physicians.

In addition there are about 300 self-help groups that use the Foundation's network to exchange the latest medical results. "Shared suffering is half the suffering." This credo motivates stroke victims and their families to meet and share their experiences, their feelings, the progress of their recovery, while exchanging information on medication, contact addresses, and tips on how to deal with doctors and insurance companies. Some members of the self-help groups socialize and go on trips together. We have noticed that stroke victims need to meet and exchange their experiences with each other. To every victim of stroke, I can only recommend joining a local self-help group. Nobody will understand you better than someone who's in the same boat. Speaking with someone else will help carry the burden and keep you motivated to look for and find new solutions for new problems. The Foundation supports contact among stroke victims by making sure that representatives from our advice and assistance department keep in touch with these groups.

I participate in self-help meetings once in a while. I always find it touching to see how energetic and motivated the victims are in their struggle with their affliction. A little while ago I met a fifty-six-year-old man who had suffered a stroke nine years earlier that had affected his center of speech. He had not been able to speak for nine months. Today, after a therapist helped him to relearn to speak like a child, he speaks well again. The only remnant of his predicament is a somewhat halting speech rhythm. His right hand is still paralyzed, but he learned to write with his left hand, and today he is even able to handle a computer with one hand. He is one of many examples that a stroke does not have to destroy your quality of life.

The foundation counts twenty-two full-time employees. The cost of the foundation's infrastructure, including personnel and administration, amounts to about 1.3 million German marks (US $650,000), carried by the Bertelsmann Foundation.

We've printed over a million pamphlets aimed at those seeking advice and those looking for information regarding prevention, treatment, and rehabilitation. We also publish a quarterly magazine with a print quantity of 45,000 copies for victims and their families. We have 15,000 sponsors whose funds go directly to specific projects.

Bertelsmann tries to set a good example by establishing preventative measures. We offered a stroke checkup to all our employees in Gütersloh, and 1,700 employees (many more than we anticipated) participated, even after working hours. The results were shocking. Twenty-five percent of those examined had to undergo medical treatment due to their high risk factors, and almost half were suffering from obesity and high blood pressure. These people will really benefit from preventive measures and will most likely be spared the suffering and dependency that goes with a stroke. Preventive measures help insurance companies, because if a stroke is prevented, they will avoid the high costs of treatment after the fact. The costs of an actual stroke amount to approximately 300,000 German marks (US $150,000) per patient per year.

Since 1995 the German Stroke Foundation has been working with several insurance companies for workers and employees to conduct an encompassing pilot study that offers regular wellness examinations to the insured. We work with the Bertelsmann insurance company and Bertelsmann AG, as well as with Deutsche Bank AG in Frankfurt, Düsseldorf, and Essen. In the near future these pilot studies will be expanded to reach Hannover.

Thus far about 5,000 people have participated, which amounts to about 20 percent of all those insured. We expect to reach another 5,000 participants by the end of the study, and hope that this is representative enough to draw general conclusions from the collected data.

According to medical statistics, about 420 of almost 5,000 participants will most likely suffer a stroke within the next ten years.

The main thing we have learned is that you can indeed motivate a great number of people to undergo goal-oriented preventive examinations. We have noticed a high occurrence of risk factors, as numerous participants of our studies belong to a high-risk group. To counteract this, a large number of participants are willing to change their behavior or to undergo medical treatment in order to reduce their risk factors. According to statistics, this would eventually reduce the probable number of actual strokes.

An important goal of this pilot study is to prove that prevention can actually reduce the cost of healthcare. Should the study produce numbers that support our assumption, the German Stroke Foundation will present its findings to political decision makers and aggressively participate in discussions on healthcare.

May 10, 1999, was our first federally recognized day for stroke awareness. In September 2000 we kicked off an entire year of programs aimed at raising awareness and preventing the occurrence of stroke. We've also planned numerous other events and media campaigns to raise awareness all over Europe. Considering that similar initiatives in the Netherlands and through the EUSI (the European Stroke Initiative) already work all over Europe, we also intend to create a European network of foundations for stroke victim assistance. Together we are strong.

When I started the Foundation in 1993, I had no idea what was in store for me. But I would do it again in an instant, because it was well worth it. The fact that I received the German Medal of Honor from President Roman Herzog for my work with the Foundation makes me very happy. It motivates me to continue on my way, because I want to be a role model for others. The honorary medal I received from the medical community this year also tells me that our Foundation's work is appreciated.

But people approaching me and thanking me means more to me than any official honor ever will. My greatest hope is that, one day, the Foundation will continue to exist and to help people without me.

11. New Responsibilities—
Corporate Culture

A little while ago I took on new responsibilities, as a partner in the Bertelsmann Asset Management Corporation, on the supervisory board of Bertelsmann AG, and on the executive board of the Bertelsmann Foundation.

The Bertelsmann Asset Management Corporation represents the capital of the company in the general stockholder meetings. According to its statutes, it consists of eight people chosen among executives, employee representatives, and family members. I will be a partner of the Asset Management Corporation until I am seventy years old, and I will fill my place with a sense of duty and responsibility toward the company. As a representative of the family it is my duty to work toward the continuation of the company's culture. The family maintains that the company's interests stand above and beyond any individual interests, in order to guarantee continuity of the Bertelsmann empire. Before I leave the Asset Management Corporation, I will appoint a family member I think will be able to fill this role after me. It will have to be someone with a great deal of experience in life and work, preferably in an executive position. After all, it is these board meetings that lay the foundation, determine the values, and support the continuity of our corporate culture.

My husband appointed me a partner of the Asset Management Corporation, and together we continue the development of the Bertelsmann corporate culture. Part of this responsibility requires that I give lectures to executives and employees in our offices in Germany and all over the world to ensure the worldwide continuity of the Bertelsmann culture.

Our special corporate culture is the basis for Bertelsmann's tremendous success. It was developed by my husband as a result of his experiences during seven years of war, three of them spent as prisoner of war with the Americans when he rebuilt the company after the war. At an age when young people today enjoy their college life, focus on self-realization, have fun, travel the world, form friendships, fall in love, get to know foreign cultures, widen their horizons, learn, and train for a career, my husband's generation was at war. They experienced death and destruction to an extent we can hardly imagine today, in a time of peace. Those who were fortunate enough to escape the inferno without physical damage still carry the psychological baggage with them for life.

Rebuilding the Company After the War

Even though his war experiences were terrible and devastating, they had a lasting positive effect. Freedom and solidarity became valuable to his personal and entrepreneurial work in a way they never would have in peacetime. He learned to value not just physical freedom, but also the freedom of thought as exemplified in America, and the unconditional cameraderie in a community where one depends on the other with his life. These were experiences he would never forget. Freedom and solidarity became his ultimate goals, goals that were to shape the house of Bertelsmann. Everything my husband did was geared toward a corporate culture adhering to the principles of partnership and a view of man free from the class structure still prevalent at the time. My husband's thinking and work was centered on his coworkers.

The employees believed in the future of our company, and their motivation and identification with the company helped build today's media empire. When, in 1946, as a young man of twenty-four years, my husband returned from the American prison camp, only one hundred of four hundred employees were left. The publishing house had been bombed just before the end of the war, and was but a heap of stones. His parents' house was occupied by British soldiers, and his father was unable to lead the company due to his asthma.

When picking up my husband at the train station, Heinrich Henke, who had been the family's driver for many years, said, "Your father is very sick. You have to manage the company now." Reinhard's oldest brother, Hans Heinrich, lovingly called "Hanger," had fallen in the first few days of the war. His younger brother, Gerd, was still a prisoner of war, and his second-oldest brother, Siegbert, remained in a Russian prison camp in Siberia until 1954. My husband was the only one available to take over.

My husband felt that he had to follow the call of family tradition, even though he'd had other professional plans. He had wanted to become an engineer. His education at home and at school had raised him to cherish discipline and duty above everything else. He had received a Protestant education, complete with regular church visits and family prayers at home. Because the family played chamber music, he had to learn to play the piano, a skill which once was an integral part of a good upbringing.

At school, by the way, he was a late bloomer. To this day he likes to remember his mother's desperation when, as a twelve-year-old, he came home with thirty mistakes on a single page of dictation. He was sent to an eye specialist to make sure that his eyesight wasn't responsible. It wasn't . . . the boy was simply weak in spelling. One day his mother was so annoyed that she suggested he should become a carpenter, because that would suit his interest in hands-on activities. He felt degraded, because all five of his siblings were good students, and he would have been the only one with a blue-collar job. So, with extreme discipline and hard work he overcame his weakness. He finished high school at the top of his class in natural sciences. This little story is meant to give hope to all parents who are close to despair over their children's grades.

When asked which skills he deems responsible for his tremendous success, my husband usually lists the following: logical thinking, people skills, decisiveness, creativity, a sense of duty, a sense of justice, and modesty. The individual's responsibility toward the community has always been important to him, because labor service[1], war, and imprisonment had taught him the value of solidarity. As a sixteen-year-old he wrote in a school essay: "I want an opportunity to contribute to the community."

He considered managing the company a personal responsibility. In addition to his work at the company, he also trained as a bookseller, and had no time to go to college. Only later would he realize that sacrificing his original professional goals created the opportunity for his professional and enterpreneurial development and personal self-realization.

The first order of business was to pick up the rubble and clean up the rust and ashes from the machines. The one hundred employees who remained trusted in and were loyal to the Bertelsmann and Mohn families, who, for four generations, had decided the fate of the company and its employees.

So, in the spring of 1946, Reinhard Mohn joined the company, not as the chief executive, but as a trainee and employee. From the outset a continuing open dialogue on questions of justice and solidarity were extremely important to him, and it was these questions that were to shape his work. During the war he had experienced the meaning of solidarity and motivation, and so he made sure that the interests of the company leadership and those of the workers would never be in opposition during the entire period of rebuilding. Later he said about this period: "We just wanted to have a roof over our heads and survive, and we knew that we had to help each other in order to achieve this. The fact that we were able to rebuild the publishing house is largely due to the commitment and knowledge of the employees who came back to work with us. They felt as much of a sense of responsibility as I did, and they made many sacrifices and worked hard.

[1] From 1935 through 1945 young boys and girls in Germany had to do mandatory work service for their city or state. This service had been a popular voluntary activity among the youth throughout Europe for several decades, but was made mandatory by the Nazi regime. The service was abolished in 1945.

Obviously the Bertelsmann tradition of one hundred years of solidarity had been successful because, just like before the war, people rallied behind their company."

Our Corporate Culture and Management Concept

Two concepts are largely responsible for the enormous rise of our company to a worldwide media empire. First, tolerance and acceptance of other cultures—we work in over fifty countries worldwide, which, especially in the field of media, requires a sensitivity in dealing with cultural differences. And second, the company's goal to contribute optimally to the democratic free enterprise of our society. To this day we believe that the company's goal above and beyond everything else is to adequately contribute to society. A company grows out of its community, receives its capital from its community, and thus should feel an obligation to give something in return. The German constitution states, "With property comes responsibility." Everyone should take this responsibility seriously above and beyond all individual goals. A company needs to create conditions in which all employees not only accept this responsibility as the higher goal, but accept it willingly and behave accordingly. For many generations the Bertelsmann and Mohn families have been committed to finding solutions for social problems within their community.

Loyalty and cooperation create relationships that are indispensable for a company, particularly in crisis situations or in situations when higher productivity is required. The employees' attitude towards their company can make or break a company's success. The house of Bertelsmann has experienced this several times over the course of its 160-year history. The continuity of the house of Bertelsmann has been saved many times by the loyalty of our employees. By the same token, the owner families always kept in touch with their employees personally and cared for their well-being. If someone was in need, the company would help out.

The house of Bertelsmann developed a corporate culture founded on freedom of thought and the principle of partnership at the heart of all management decisions. Postwar society is now populated by democratic citizens with high demands on their lives. Today's employees need to believe in their work, and they demand a chance to prove themselves both in their lives and in their work. Therefore all employees need to be able to identify with the company for which they work; its goals, its philosophy, and its responsibilities. Only a wide leadership pyramid and co-operation based on partnership makes this possible. All company achievements need to be presented as joint efforts. My husband realized that it was no longer possible to lead a company solely according to patriarchal principles, but that it is necessary to del-egate responsibility. The corporate culture he built is based on the principles of partnership, a modern leadership style centered on the modern self-confident employee.

A changed view of man is largely responsible for this. The process of democratization after the war, better education, and a higher standard of living have changed the way individuals see themselves, along with the goals and expectations they set for their lives. While historically only the entrepreneur strived for self-realization in his work, today every single employee goes to work expecting much more than merely securing his financial needs. It is the desire to define work as a meaningful part of life that makes today's employees choose their professions.

An atmosphere ruled by order and obedience, no matter how finely tuned, no longer suits today's economic world, because it stifles initiative and ultimately fosters utter disinterest. If an em-ployee receives only orders, the sense of freedom disappears and gives way to fear. Unmotivated employees do only what's neces-sary and don't feel any commitment. Their creativity suffocates. A successful corporation needs leaders who think and work like middle-class entrepreneurs, leaders who are in tune with what's going on with the workforce.

A modern corporation does not have room for an authoritarian style of leadership. Authority doesn't come with a particular position, but rather from a particular personality, one that motivates by showing professionalism and the ability to dissipate employee frustrations. A true leader must present goals, show vision, motivate, make, and evaluate decisions. A leader should not give orders, but communicate and cooperate with his colleagues. A leader needs to look for and find consensus, not by ramming through decisions without his employees, but by forming and implementing these decisions in cooperation with his employees. A leader must inspire those he leads. A leader must trust those he leads. True harmony sets energy free, as much as true humanity creates efficiency.

My husband believes in teaching employees to think like entrepreneurs by letting them make decisions and mistakes, for the best way to learn is from mistakes. My husband believes that this is much more efficient than having the board make all the decisions. But, of course, you have to learn to think creatively, and allowing your employees to do so may result in a change of corporate culture. And, in addition, not all employees are equipped with entrepreneurial creativity. My husband usually makes this point with an example from his POW days at a can factory, where he filled cans of tomatoes on an assembly line. While he found it terribly boring, some of POWs seemed rather content with it. Some people find satisfaction in performing repetitive activity with others. If you had told these people to start thinking on their own, they wouldn't have wanted to. Only a certain percentage of employees is willing and able to develop entrepreneurial skills. Not everyone can show maximum performance.

The leadership skills that will count in the future go far beyond knowledge, to include creative talents, self-motivation, and entrepreneurial vision. While a college education is very valuable, only practical training in business and economy will teach and test any given employee's entrepreneurial skills. This is learning by doing, which is especially valuable for developing people skills. Rather than capital and work, it is the ability of top executives to lead and manage their employees who will steer the economic future of a society. We need to give the untapped potential of employees' creativity a chance to develop.

Investment in people promises success; not only is it necessary, but it is the best way to guarantee the continuity of a company. Our corporation has always stressed the importance of the search, selection, and support of employees with leadership potential worldwide.

When selecting an employee with leadership potential, personality is more important than grades. For some time my husband has been interested in graphology, and he always requests handwriting evaluations of important potential colleagues. This method is impressively precise in the evaluation of a personality. Over the years we have developed so much knowledge in graphology that often a glance at someone's handwriting is enough to judge a person's character. It's a great way to determine whether or not someone will be up to a specific task.

The house of Bertelsmann created a department devoted exclusively to the development of our managers and executives. The department offers about twenty corporate training seminars on topics concerning leadership. Group leaders, shift leaders, executives-in-training, and members of the board participate in equal numbers. For example, the department offers basic classes in subjects such as management skills, project management, negotiation skills, and operating within the Bertelsmann leadership structure. If desired, we also advise individual managers at all levels on improving their own personal leadership style, developing self-motivational skills, conflict resolution skills, as well as offering help in any difficult situation.

Our principles of leadership—we call them The Ten Commandments—prescribe that executives must give the employees they supervise responsibility for their assignments, along with the necessary information for those assignments. Executives are also encouraged to accept ideas and criticism, discuss goals openly, and acknowledge achievements in order to understand the individual empoyee's motivational situation. All our executives-in-training learn that a leader is a role model, one who cares for his employees.

The skills and abilities a manager or entrepreneur should exhibit are:

- professionalism and knowledge
- honesty
- the ability to work under pressure
- productivity
- strength of character
- composure
- communication skills
- a sense of right and wrong
- decisiveness
- straightforwardness
- an ability to evaluate entrepreneurial goals and responsibilities.

A manager should not exhibit the following:

- vanity
- disloyalty and distrust
- dishonesty (basis for termination)
- intrigue and partisanship
- a lust for power.

Of course, even a company governed by the principle of partnership will experience conflict. Constructive and critical discourse among executives and between executives and employees is imperative to remain productive and competitive. If a company resolves conflicts and discusses problems based on the positive characteristics named above, a sense of teamwork develops, which in turn serves as a basis for mutual economic success.

The Delegation of Responsibility—
Decentralization

Delegating responsbility to lower levels allows a company to tap into a great potential of productivity and creativity. At the same time, delegating responsibility builds bridges and fosters coopera-tion and communication at the workplace. If we are able to mo-tivate our employees to think and to make their own decisions, everyone involved will enjoy work more, and the companies will profit due to higher employee achievement, fewer mistakes, and better quality of work. Obviously, a company's success will follow.

Consider the results of a study among retirees in this context: An employee who learned to think and act for himself at his workplace has no trouble finding meaningful activities alone or with others during retirement. On the other hand, employees who haven't been allowed to make their own decisions during their professional lives didn't know how to do so in old age ei-ther. Those people enjoy life less and, as expereince shows, age faster as well.

At Bertelsmann we believe that executives need to respond quickly and creatively to new situations, and so we decentralize and delegate, because the responsible executives need entrepre-neurial freedom, including the right to learn from their mistakes in order to grow. The word *entrepreneur* comes from *enterprise*. It is only when you don't engage in enterprises that you never make mistakes, and that is the biggest mistake of all. Decentralization means flexibility. Quick response and efficiency allow creative and innovative thinking, which in turn allows great achieve-ments and high productivity in our competitive and ever-changing market. The global economy offers great opportunities, yet demands that we meet ever-new challenges and withstand growing pressures. There's never been a greater challenge in history.

Many entrepreneurs and executives think that delegating re-ponsibility means a loss of image and power. The thought that other people's opinions might be worthwhile is terrible, even unthinkable for many of them. Many executives are unable to communicate. But when a company grows quickly, executives cannot be the ones to make all the decisions. If a company has too many strict rules, the decision-making process becomes bureaucratic and inflexible, which ultimately hinders the company's competitiveness. Many large corporations believe that through central leadership and a mass of rules they can avoid mistakes. They believe that their employees are not able to solve problems on their own. Such distrust stifles the democratic learning process.

Our old and rusty structures in public services, the government, and administration are an excellent example of this. I think it is very important for the government to be led by principles of partnership. People would be more motivated, more productive, and more efficient, and everyone would save a lot of money.

Communication and Dialogue

If you don't talk to your employees, if you don't ask for their opinion, if you don't believe that they may have great skills, you'll never find out what they may achieve. An American entrepreneur once put it quite succinctly: "Let many heads think, and a company is very rich."

Acknowledge the experience and knowledge of your employees, appreciate their personalities, let them know that they are not just cogs in the machine, and they will strive to think outside the box and will come up with innovative concepts they otherwise never would have thought of. Communicating in an atmosphere of trust makes it much easier to discuss new ideas and find solutions for difficult problems.

Bertelsmann took this to heart and developed a system of interviews and dialogues. Every five years we conduct anonymous interviews among employees regarding our corporate culture, the leadership style of supervisors, and advancement possibilities. The employees fill out a questionnaire on their job and working conditions, the level of cooperation with their direct supervisor, their level of satisfaction with their supervisor, colleagues, and the company's climate, and the status of their education and development opportunities. The results of the questionnaire are evaluated on the executive level and then openly discussed within the departments, with the support of executives, personnel, and employee representation. Together we can make a change. According to a study, 80 percent of our employees find the questionnaire important to very important.

A good executive has certain demands on his or her career. To be able to meet them, we conduct regular conversations to make sure an executive's professional future develops in a way that is mutually satisfactory. Managers and their supervisors speak with one another annually to create a personal productivity profile complete with strengths and weaknesses, and to advise executives on their developmental opportunities and professional goals. These talks evaluate the achievements of the past year and define goals for the coming year.

Every employee can have a conversation annually with his or her supervisor. Away from daily pressures, employee and supervisor discuss the work situation and take into account what has been achieved and where there is room for improvement. The supervisor assesses the employee's work in the past year. Of course, the employee is encouraged to express his or her opinion as well. The conversation is intended to investigate how an employee's responsibilities could be changed to improve individual professional achievements. What can the supervisor do to improve working conditions and to make cooperation more efficient? Does the employee need to participate in educational programs, or should a particular job description be modified so that the individual might achieve more? Sometimes, of course, it is also necessary to acknowledge and set limits. To do so it is often necessary to use sensitive and constructive criticism. It is the duty of the supervisor to take responsibility for his employee, because to lead is to protect and to care.

Sometimes, however, an employee must find out for himself

where his or her limits are. The ability to understand what you can and cannot do is a form of self-realization as well. This may create great anxiety and test your limits, but this is how you'll know what you can take and what you can do. I know what I am talking about, because I've experienced it myself.

During our "January talks" employees evaluate their supervisors. Every January, we hold a group meeting between supervisors and their departments, in which employees are encouraged to tell their managers what they think about their work. These talks discuss the level of cooperation, possible work flow improvements, and the general climate within the department. One of the most important questions in these talks is to ask the employee how the supervisor might contribute to greater job satisfaction. Sometimes such a group conversation is the starting point for an individual talk. Corporate management recommends these January talks highly.

My employees and I conduct these evaluation talks not only in January, but frequently throughout the year. Positive and constructive criticism after an event—what worked and what didn't—is part of it.

I think I am very fair with my employees. I want to help them as much as I can, but I also think that they have to help me as much as they can. I often say that we all depend on each other. I conduct such conversations regularly, in groups large and small. I ask about specific needs or desires, but I also mention my own needs and desires. It is important to me that everyone knows that we are a team working together toward success. Part of this is that we are all having fun doing it. We deal with each other fairly and openly and show respect for each other. Everyone has an important contribution in his particular place. Everybody needs the opportunity to make something of his life.

This system is designed to create transparency and openness from the bottom up as well as from the top down. Mutual openness is the only way to make productive and unburdened cooperation possible. Mutual understanding and communication is the only way to create the energy required for a common goal.

Intrigue, back-stabbing or strategizing, jealous competitiveness, and envy take too much energy away from the work of the company. It won't help anyone.

I am happy every time I hear that my employees are happy. This inspires me to continue on my path.

Our international excutives-in-training (about fifty young people) meet in Hamburg, Gütersloh, Paris, New York, and Kitzbühel. They work together during the day, and in the evening they get to know each other over dinner. This is how the sense of togetherness so typical of our corporation grows. We are all "Bertelsmen" and "Bertelswomen". We believe that a phone call or an e-mail cannot replace personal contact. Even in the exciting world of new media we cannot do without a personal connection. You've got to look a person in the eye in order to see and evaluate his or her whole personality. It is more human and more efficient.

As part of the continuing open dialogue within our corporation, assistants of the board of directors from all over the world meet annually in our headquarters in Gütersloh. I initiated these meetings because I find it very important that these employees get to know one another personally while sharing professional experiences. At every meeting one of us gives a lecture on a current issue, and board members or executives offer presentations on their division's goals and achievements. Daily communication becomes so much easier if this important circle of people has a personal connection. Work flow would be much more difficult if these people didn't know each other. The experience of assistants in the day-to-day operations of the company often leads to innovative personnel development of the corporation. Over the years this forum has laid the groundwork for improved communication and is an integral part of our corporate culture. As we care for our leaders and managers, we care for their secretaries and assistants.

And, by the way, this dialogue-based structure helps in the dealings between tariff partners, as it changes the adversarial nature of the dispute to one that is more cooperative.

The Bertelsmann "Fall talk," in particular, shows how important the dialogue, the search for solutions, and the ongoing exchange between the executive level and the employee committee[2] really is. In urgent cases the head of the employee committee doesn't have to wait until autumn, but can contact the chairman of the board or me directly. Constructive dialogue without any rough edges requires a groundwork of mutual trust and loyalty. So far there has not been a single case where the employee committee misused this for petty issues, disloyalty or presented a strictly confrontational attitude.

Motivation and Identification

Creativity, vision, motivation, and personnel management are the skills required for the future.

The sense of freedom created by delegating responsibility requires that every employee identify with the general goal of the company. Clearly defined goals, a specific leadership concept, and a fair compensation scale form the basis for employee motivation. Employee commitment is the key to our success as a company based on the principle of partnership. The house of Bertelsmann realizes that responsibility and freedom create motivation. Identification and creativity increase the productivity of our employees. They want to achieve things, and our executives support them in that.

In accordance with its corporate culture, the house of Bertelsmann has installed computers with Internet access in the homes of all of its 65,000 employees. We put aside 100 million German marks (US $50 million) for this purpose. Access to the data network gives each employee the opportunity for continuing their education, and also plugs them into the future. In addi-

[2] Within every company the employees form a committee that represents their interests. The leaders of this committee are often present at board meetings to make sure that employees' interests are respected in the decision-making process. These committees are required by law and are an integral part of all union activities.

tion, this program will also foster identification with the corporation as well.

Profit-sharing programs increase the employees' sense of responsibility, motivation, and identification. Since 1970, Bertelsmann has practiced the equal distribution of profits. Every investor receives a minimum advance of dividends from the corporation's profits in regular and automatic payments similar to that of salaries, which are paid in advance as well. Any additional profits are divided equally between investors and employees, although the amount distributed to each employee is contingent upon salary. The motivation behind this is greater financial equity. We've had positive results so far, because profit sharing fosters employee interest and provides insight into and understanding of economic issues.

We offer our leadership personnel attractive entrepreneurial working conditions. They are entrepreneurs within the enterprise, and participate in the corporation's success through stock options for exceptional achievements. We also encourage executives to invest in their own divisions.

The quality and creativity of our employees depend directly on their level of motivation. Well-led companies have fewer sick days. It is a well-known fact that organizations that do not incorporate principles of partnership in their leadership are partially responsible for a high volume of sick days, whereas modern leadership styles based on employee participation show a decrease in sick days. This presents a new beginning for corporate health plans; a motivated and committed employee takes fewer sick days.

A company that places concern for the employee at the center is in itself an adequate health program. Entrepreneurs and executives should consider this. Here are a few comparative numbers: German public sector absenteeism due to health considerations may average up to 29 days annually; in the private sector these numbers drop to an average of 10 to 11; and at Bertelsmann to fewer than 9 days, sometimes as few as a day and a half per year. It's not that these people are sick less often, they are simply more motivated.

Research has shown that strategizing and harrassment at the workplace is expensive for insurance companies and employers. The AOK[2] in Bavaria estimated that each case costs the insurance company between 30,000 and 100,000 German marks (between US $15,000 and US $50,000) in treatment. It is not always the obvious illness that affects the physical well-being of an employee, but also the wearing down of one's psyche and morale. In other words, an employee's sick day may have hidden reasons: poor working conditions, an antisocial working climate, too many or too few demands at the workplace, a lack of information and opportunities to influence one's work, or strained relationships between supervisors and employees.

These problems are avoided by incorporating partnership concepts into the corporate culture. Fewer sick days are not only good for the individual, but for the entire corporation, and, ultimately, for the whole of society. Incredible amounts of health-care funds could be saved if we had fewer sick days.

My Personal Leadership Style

To lead is to serve and to do good.

When selecting colleagues to work closely with me, I make certain that the applicant is a good match, not only with me personally, but with our other colleagues and with the company culture in general. I often ask for a second interview, sometimes over dinner, to get acquainted with the applicant, to explain our work flow in detail, and to learn more about the person's etiquette. I feel the need to have a clear picture of the applicant, because in my area it's particularly important.

---

[2] The AOK (*Allgemeine Ortskrankenkasse*) is a public health insurance company with local offices all over Germany.

I carefully observe people's behavior and performance. I don't accept tricks or cheating. My leadership style depends on the delegation of responsibility, which requires that I trust my employees and that they, in turn, behave professionally. My trust in an employee is proven when I, as their supervisor, say, "Here's your chance, do something with it." Is there any stronger motivation for great achievements than a common goal, satisfying work conditions, the opportunity to develop new ideas, and being successful as a team?

I do my best to treat everyone around me fairly. Praise is an important leadership tool with which to motivate employees. If possible, criticism should take place only in private so that the employee won't lose face. And it's important to look for solutions and ways to improve together.

I also expect a strong work ethic from my colleagues, including a sense of commitment, flexibility, discipline, and the willingness to engage in ongoing communication.

Every new project my department undertakes is first discussed by my entire team. As an example, consider the topic of nutrition. We would first discuss which questions to tackle, and which questions would be most current. Should we research the nutrition of children, perhaps with a focus on the rise of allergic reactions? Or should we investigate the nutrition of the elderly who so often suffer from deficiencies? One of us might suggest researching the nutrition offered in nationwide school and company cafeterias. These discussions require constant give and take. I appreciate every good suggestion, and I push an idea through if I believe in it.

Of course, in your professional life you might have to deal with an employee who may not feel well or has problems. As long as you speak about it openly, such situations can be handled efficiently. I am sensitive, so I can often tell immediately if someone doesn't feel well. Whenever I can, I try to give advice and offer help. I can tell by the employee's reaction to my expressions of concern whether or not they want to talk. I ask them into my office and ask about their troubles, and often we end up having a very candid conversation. In offering help and advice in any given situation, I try to draw from my own experiences. If I find out that a family member is in the hospital, or that someone in the family is ill or has had an accident, I try to arrange for optimal care.

Recently, for example, one of my assistants was greatly worried about her sister. The young woman was suffering from recurring rheumatism, and no therapy seemed to help. I immediately called a specialist I knew and arranged for the young woman to meet him. And indeed, the specialist had a new therapy that eased her pain. I was very happy to receive her thank-you note and flowers, but the greatest gift was simply having been able to help.

There are some personal conversations one needs to handle with great sensitivity. Relationship or family problems, for example, cannot be addressed directly, because someone might get hurt. But even on these issues my own personal experiences often allow me to give advice and support.

My colleagues also notice when I don't feel well or when I'm under a lot of stress. In these situations we understand each other without words, and my colleagues say so with small gestures. Or if there's a work-related emergency, my personal assistant Martin Spilker reassures me with a simple "We'll take care of that." This is how we support one another.

Once in a while I'll go to dinner with my colleagues to exchange thoughts on a more personal level, far from the daily grind. We get to know each other better and we become closer. This in turn will increase the sense of togetherness at work. I love these spontaneous outings.

My husband works closely with his colleagues as well. He usually has lunch in the cafeteria, not just at the executive table, but among assistants and secretaries, his and mine. This often surprises guests from outside the company, but his colleagues are happy. In his distinct voice and with his unique sense of humor he might even entertain his colleagues with a few anecdotes.

Talk to one another—that's our recipe. If people talk to one another, life at work is easier.

Our belief in humanity and our sense of justice and solidarity have established channels of communiction that are always open in the house of Bertelsmann, and that fosters a corporate structure based on the principle of partnership. This increases the stability, competitiveness, and adaptablity of a company. It is not only the experience of Bertelsmann, but of numerous other companies worldwide as well.

Partnership in this context means:

- mutual understanding and cooperation
- a commitment to learning through ongoing two-way communication
- employee participation
- meaningful work
- a company's sense of social responsibility
- humanity wins!

The Bertelsmann Essentials

The following are a few values adhered to by our owners, executives, and employees alike:

Our mission: We distribute information, education, and entertainment all over the world. It is our goal to contribute to the productivity of society. We strive to be leaders in our markets. We want to create a just and motivating working environment.

Our basic values:

Partnership is the basis of our corporate culture. To serve our employees and the company as a whole, the following principles guide us: respect for the individual, mutual trust, and the delegation of responsibility. We make sure our employees receive adequate information, are included in the decision-making process, and are able to partake in the economic success of the corporation. The compensation of our employees mirrors their personal contribution as well as our company's productivity. Our company seeks to secure long-term employment.

Identification and motivation: We believe that individuals strive for freedom and self-realization, and therefore we trust in the individual's initiative and creativity. Motivated individuals who identify with the company, its goals, and values are an engine for quality, efficiency, and growth. Information, communication, and active participation build the foundation for identification and motivation.

Entrepreneurial spirit: We encourage all employees to accept complete responsibility for any given assignment. They are to behave as entrepreneurs, combining inventiveness, creativity, and energy with a sense of responsibility to strive for ultimate achievements.

Decentralization: This is the key to our success. The individual Bertelsmann companies are given as much freedom as possible.

Cooperation: With entrepreneurial freedom comes the responsibility to work together in a constructive manner. Executives must ensure that their activities do not just benefit the individual company, but support the interests of the entire corporation and of our partners in other companies as well.

Employee development: We invest in our employees and offer equal opportunities contingent upon their abilities and performance. We support our employees above and beyond the limits of their function, country, or product lines. We want to attract the best, most creative enterpreneurial talents and specialists in all fields. The training of future corporate leadership is considered a contribution to the corporation's continuity.

Diversity of content: Our program allows for a pluralism of opinions and attitudes. Each individual company develops its own content profile. We guarantee artistic freedom and freedom of speech. We support democracy and human rights all over the world, while respecting the traditions and values of each country in which we do business.

Ethics: Our companies honor law and order and are guided by the highest ethical standards. We expect every single employee to do his or her job according to these ethical principles. We disapprove of any and all discrimination and harassment in the workplace. We expect every single one of our employees to behave responsibly toward their colleagues, community, and environment.

Contribution to the community: We are convinced that our corporate activities and publishing goals contribute to the common good. We accept the special responsibility that comes with the nature of the media and with economic success. Like all good citizens, our companies are committed to the communities in which they work.

I believe that the Bertelsmann corporation is always aware of its responsibility toward society.

12. A New Era

Our daily life changes faster than ever before, and our society is undergoing incredible transformations. Technical innovations, the Internet, globalization, stock market exuberance, mergers—old structures are crumbling. News travels the world in seconds, information flows freely. The working world is experiencing a fundamental change, moving out of the Industrial Age and into the Information Age. Production has lost its leading role, while knowledge and management have taken its place. We learn more, and we learn more quickly in order to stay competitive, and many people are overwhelmed by that. Larger, faster, farther, richer—and all it costs us is our sense of security. These are the characteristics of the new global epoch.

There are many questions:

- Are our social and economic goals still realistic?
- Should we revisit our goals and adapt them to the latest developments?
- Will our economic, political, and social leadership be able to meet the new challenges?
- Will the government and administration be able to work productively?
- Will we be able to combine a competitive edge with a lasting sense of humanity?
- What do we need to learn and do in order to keep up with these developments?

We don't have the answers to any of these questions.

In a world in which we don't know if today's profession will

will pay tomorrow's bills, in which we don't know where we will work tomorrow, in which we need to be mobile, flexible, and willing to move in an instant, human connections and relationships become more and more important. Such relationships promise stability in a changing environment that can seem beyond our control. It is vitally important not to lose our ethical orientation in such a world. Universal ethical values can provide inner strength and independence. Our only chance to counteract the breakdown of society are values such as responsibility, honesty, decency, fairness, tolerance, humanity, compassion, and solidarity with the weak. These values are the compass that should direct our lives.

Our world is defined by materialsim and egotism, yet, in the long run, people need more than mere material values. Economic factors alone will not be able to motivate us, for material goods cannot replace the warmth that comes with love and humanity.

We need acceptable and accepted rules for our life within the community. We need to clarify which goals we want to achieve, because a mere conglomeration of knowledge will not create a worldwide community based on the principle of solidarity. We need to develop and nurture the willingness to do what's responsible. Where will we end up if everyone just does as he pleases? A society acting according to this principle will eventually dissolve. The challenge of the twenty-first century will be handling the need for new goals and rules.

The new media, as well as science and technology, offer great opportunities. The working world has changed, for employees are no longer mere recipients of orders; hierarchies and central leadership modes have become obsolete, while employee participation offers a chance to be creative. Strict working hours and lifelong employment relationships will fade away, and in their stead we will live with more flexible working arrangements.

On the other hand, it will be possible to collect overtime and credit it to "lifelong work accounts" over the years, the dividend being early retirement[1].

When we delegate responsibility, we'll do so based on the idea that, while the work has to be done, it is left up to the employee's discretion to decide when and how. Modern means of communication make it possible to live as freely as ever before. Will we be able to manage this freedom responsibly?

Professions disappear, and new professional profiles take their place. Young people begin their careers in Germany, continue on to New York, and end in Hong Kong. Are we adequately equipped to meet the demands and opportunities of global competition? Even though we are doing better than earlier generations, young people today are faced with unparalleled pressures and demands. You need to be strong if you don't want to merely hunt for material success that has no soul.

We have to take responsibility for ourselves, for the weak, and for our society as a whole. Even the young winners of the Internet's dot-com world who became millionaires overnight need to exhibit a sense of responsibility to guide them. With property comes responsibility—this is true for these young entrepreneurs as well. They shouldn't ignore their responsibility toward their community.

The world is growing together. Every product and piece of information can be purchased anywhere at any time. Will the different cultures of the world be able to adapt to this, or will the development of a global culture destroy individual cultural identities? These are questions that will decide the course of our future. When Bill Clinton suggested supporting high-speed

---

[1] German companies are exploring more flexible working arrangements for their employees, among them so-called *Lebensarbeitskonten* (lifelong work accounts). These accounts would allow employees to collect overtime throughout their working life. Rather than losing their overtime if it is not redeemed within a certain time frame or while working for a particular company, the time can be credited to these accounts to be redeemed in the form of early retirement.

economic and cultural developments during the World Economic Forum, he didn't understand that adequately dealing with change requires time. Otherwise people will lose their cultural roots, which will have unknown effects on society as a whole.

The chasm between rich and poor countries will grow. It has only been eleven years since the fall of the Iron Curtain in Europe, and already we are in the middle of a new migration. Do we really have to build new walls to fight against this onslaught of people? Nelson Mandela so rightly states, "Poverty creates violence and crime." It is urgent that Western countries teach countries with a lower gross national product to help themselves.

On the other hand, scientists tell us that Europe will need more and more new immigrants in the future. So we must learn to see immigrants as an enrichment to our culture, and, by the same token, immigrants living among us need to be willing to adapt. This is a difficult process that will require tolerance.

Many people are overwhelmed by the flood of information coming toward us every single day. We have to learn to deal with, and select from, an immense amount of information. We have to handle technology; technology cannot be allowed to handle us. The Internet is an instrument we can and must use. Knowledge alone is no longer enough, and it is no longer important where you get your informaton. What is important is how you sort and organize the information, and how you manage it while retaining your decisiveness. The ability to select important information quickly will make or break an individual's success.

The Internet, with its millions of e-mails a day, seems to be beyond all control. It offers instructions on how to build bombs and how to create dynamite, and you can find pornography for every sexual persuasion. A culture of deceit and crime grows within the Internet's anonymity, for the responsible persons cannot be held accountable. It goes without saying that this threatens peace in our society.

We may even end up living second-hand lives, for the huge freedom we've won may actually lead us into utter loneliness. If we don't ever leave our houses because the world comes to us via computer, virtual communication will create an existence that is cut off from human togetherness and caring. How will we cope with that? Do we really want this? My answer is a resounding "No"!

How will we deal with the elderly? People live longer than ever before. In Germany alone there are seven thousand people over one hundred, and eighty thousand people are over ninety-five. After childhood, schooling, and professional life, people can live a long, active, and healthy fourth phase of life in retirement. Society has to be prepared for this. Health and retirement systems are strongly affected by these demographic developments. We need to find solutions that guarantee our retirees a joyful and dignified life into their old age. We need to develop models for age-appropriate living, because too many retirees are forced to live in undignified circumstances.

Responsibility and the sense of community are at the center of the coming century.

Knowledge may be power, but knowledge alone cannot determine the fight between good and evil. We can only meet the challenges of our future if we pay more attention to others and their interests. Survival of the fittest can no longer be the governing principle of our society. True leadership requires the proven ability to manage people along with a true commitment to goals geared toward the common good.

Final Thesis

What does mankind and our society need today and in the future?

Family: The family is the bedrock of our community. A family means love and comfort. The state cannot replace family relationships.

Cultural roots: They don't change as quickly as some might think. Rituals, traditions, and a sense of belonging provide orientation and stability in a world of constant change.

Children: Children guarantee the survival of a society. A goal-oriented education should not be neglected, as it is important for the intellectual and emotional development of children.

Religion: Faith provides stability, advice, and help in good times and bad and is necessary to a great number of people.

Responsibility: Only a sense of responsibility for yourself and others will further the development of solidarity among free citizens. The government cannot carry the burden of caring for all citizens by itself.

Politics: Political leaders need to make decisions. It is their task to act in the interest of citizens within the rules of democracy.

Ethical education: A sense of ethics will create and justify trust among people. Trust is the basis of togetherness and cooperation. A lack of reliability destroys trust.

Delegation of responsibility: The delegation of responsibility changes the view of man. The patriarchal principle of leadership is obsolete. Hierarchies must be dismantled.

Tolerance: We need to learn tolerance in order to cope with the problems of modern migration. Immigrants have the right and the duty to strive for integration.

Developing communication: Consensus is the indispensable prerequisite for the ability to act in our society.

Solidarity: Solidarity holds a society together. Self-realization must be tempered by a sense of limits.

Belief in the benevolence of man: This is as necessary as it is to support others, and to accept others with all their weaknesses.

Love and humanity: Both remain the ideals upon which to base a society which will be able and willing to learn and adapt in the whirlpool of change.

It is a worthwhile path: *Love opens hearts!*

"Life full of suffering and love is better than time without the sun and the wind."
Agnes Seipel, 1889–1978, mother of Reinhard Mohn

Photo Sources